Western Frontiersmen Series

XV

JOHN SIMPSON SMITH AT CAMP SUPPLY, 1869

Smith, full bearded, stands fourth from left in this 1869 photograph at Camp Supply. On his right is Romero, guide-interpreter for Custer's Washita Expedition. On his left, Brinton Darlington, Quaker founder of the Darlington Agency.

Courtesy, Muriel Wright, Oklahoma Historical Society

The Western Odyssey
of
JOHN SIMPSON SMITH

Frontiersman, Trapper
Trader, and Interpreter

by
STAN HOIG

THE ARTHUR H. CLARK COMPANY
Glendale, California
1974

To my mother
KATHLEEN KEEVER HOIG

Contents

Illustrations

Foreword

A full century has passed now since the death of John Simpson Smith. Unlike many of his comrades—men such as Kit Carson, Tom Fitzpatrick, William Bent, James Beckwourth, and others—John S. Smith failed to be remembered for the important role he played in the early West.

Perhaps it was the name he bore, possibly the most common of all American names and adopted by many who came West and wished to hide their real identities. Perhaps, it was because he was identified with the Indian at a time in history when that native American was bitterly hated by the frontier military and by immigrant settlers. Or perhaps it was simply that he stayed too long, outliving his time of historical pertinence.

Whatever the reason, Smith fully deserves a recognized place in Western history. Garrard's *Wah-to-Yah and the Taos Trail*, truly a classic of the early West, first introduced Smith to the American reading public in 1848 and painted a living picture of the frontiersman as he traded among the Cheyennes along the Arkansas River. But Smith was only thirty-six years of age then, and the American West was still a wilderness and beautifully content. Ahead lay years of conflict, and much was yet to happen in the life of John S. Smith.

It is important, however, that his story be told for reasons other than to acknowledge his existence. Smith represented the very few Americans who ever fully understood the American Indian. Public opinion of his day was generally characterized by the blind benevolence of the Eastern "olive brancher" or the equally blind hatred of frontier settlers and military men. That same polarization of views concerning the Indian continues in the literature of the West today, and it is to be hoped that the life story of John Smith can lend realistic insight to the subject.

I wish to acknowledge the help of many people in the preparation of this book, especially the following: Mrs. Alice Timmons, University of Oklahoma library; Mr. Jack Haley, University of Oklahoma Division of Manuscripts; Dr. Arrell M. Gibson, University of Oklahoma History Department; Mrs. Rella Looney, Oklahoma State Historical Society; Mr. Charles Roundy, Western History Research Center, University of Wyoming; Mrs. Agnes Wright Spring, Colorado State Historical Society; Mrs. Alys Freeze, Western History Department, Denver Public Library; Mr. Robert Richmond, Kansas State Historical Society; my wife, Pat Corbell Hoig, for her great help in proofreading and preparation of this work; and Mrs. Sally Richards for her expert typing.

Preface

The story is told that when President Andrew Johnson once visited St. Louis and was pointed out to the frontier-famous Jim Bridger, the old scout snorted in disgust and replied:

"Hell, you can't fool me. That's old John Smith!"

The resemblance of John Simpson Smith to a president of the United States is interesting, but of less consequence than the fact that Smith was well known to Jim Bridger and to countless other famous people of nineteenth century America, including presidents, congressmen, generals, governors, explorers, Indian chiefs, and a multitude of persons who took part in the wondrous drama of the American West.

Once listed in the *Encyclopaedia Britannica,* Smith has all but faded from public memory, though the records, diaries, memoirs, official Army and Indian Bureau reports, and histories of the American West are replete with mention of him. His reputation was never glorified to the extent that were those of Carson, Bridger, Fitzpatrick, Bent and others, but he was more involved in the developments of the Central Plains between 1830 and 1871 than any other one man.

Smith's place in history could easily be established in any of a variety of activities: as one of the early mountain men fur trappers; as a Bent's Fort trader; as a white man who lived for more than thirty years in close proximity to

the Cheyenne and Arapaho Indians; as the official government interpreter to the four major treaties with those
tribes—Fort Laramie in 1851, Fort Wise in 1861, the Little Arkansas in 1865, and Medicine Lodge in 1867; as an
advisor to every one of the Indian agents for those tribes
during his lifetime—Fitzpatrick, Whitfield, Miller, Bent,
Boone, Colley, Wynkoop, Taylor, and Darlington; as a
witness to most of the major conflicts between the Indians
of the Central Plains and the white man; as an Army scout
and guide; as an escort to three different delegations of
chiefs to Washington where he interpreted for Presidents
Fillmore, Lincoln, and Grant; as a friend and advisor to
virtually all of the Cheyenne and Arapaho chiefs of his
day, especially the Cheyenne peacemaker, Black Kettle;
as the one man through whom passed most of the important dialogue between the Cheyenne and the white man
during those crucial days of conflict on the Central Plains.

Smith's influence upon the policies of both military
leader and Indian agent was pronounced. He was the recognized authority and spokesman on affairs affecting the
Cheyenne and Arapaho Indians. On hundreds of occasions
over a period of thirty years he was the voice by which the
Cheyenne heard the white man and the white man heard
the Cheyenne. His counsel was listened to and followed
on many occasions by the chiefs of the tribes, just as it was
by many of the military and Indian Affairs people. In all
things Cheyenne, he was considered the most knowledge-
able, and it was he who assisted Schoolcraft in first writing down the Cheyenne and the Arapaho vocabularies.

Beyond his influencial services as an interpreter, Smith
played an important role as the principal trader to the
Cheyennes and Arapahoes. Through him the tribes were
provided with the many goods of the white man which
they needed and desired. The Indian trade itself was cru-

cial to the peace and welfare of the Plains Indians, and
Smith must be ranked with Bridger, Chisholm, and Bent
in that respect.

Nor was there anyone, white or Indian, who was better
acquainted with the country from the Upper Missouri of
Montana to the Red River of Texas. He knew virtually all
of the trails, the hunting ranges, the rivers, the Indian
tribes, and camping grounds of that vast region. The early
forts with which he is known to have been associated
include Union, Pierre, MacKenzie, Laramie, Bent's, St.
Vrain, Lupton, Lyon, Larned, Adobe, Mann, Atkinson,
Dodge, Harker, Hays, Kearny, Zarah, and Supply.

Smith played an active part in the early histories of
Missouri, Kansas, Nebraska, Wyoming, Montana, Colorado, Texas, and Oklahoma. His expertise on the geography and the nature of the Central Plains was called upon
many times by early explorers such as Fremont; by immigrants to Oregon; by gold-rushers to California, Utah, and
Colorado; by military officers wishing to contact the
tribes; by Indian agents delivering annuity goods to them;
and others.

Despite all of this, it would be a mistake to build a pure
hero image of John S. Smith. He was altogether human,
capable of both bravery and practical discretion. The simple fact that he managed to survive over forty years in the
wilderness of Western America is testimony to his adapt-
ability, shrewdness, and capacity for survival. As Garrard
pointed out in *Wah-to-Yah*, Smith, like other mountain
men, was a contradiction.

He could be both mean and kind, rough and gracious,
savage and civilized. He was a proven friend to the Indian,
yet it was not beyond him to assist Colley in trading the
Indians their own annuity goods. He was a close friend to
Black Kettle and a son-in-law to Yellow Wolf, yet he

aided the Army in campaigns against the warring Dog Soldiers. His treatment of his Indian wives, of which he had several, was Indian-style and left considerable room for improvement.

Like most men, Smith had his enemies, particularly among the second-generation of frontier military, who considered him to be a bad influence on the Indians, and among the Indian-hating settlers who despised "squaw-men" in general for their association with the Indians. Some considered him to be an unscrupulous profiteer and one who incited the tribes to war. He was neither, but Smith was placed in a difficult position when troubles between white and red men arose.

He knew the Cheyenne well—as a noble race, loving, honorable by their own code, a good friend to the white man during the early years, brave beyond description, yet a barbaric being whose war culture was fated to bring self-destruction in the face of the overwhelming wash of the white man's civilization.

The old chiefs could see this with him, but the hot-blooded young warriors who had not yet won their place in the sun would not bend to that valid but unhappy truth. To them Smith was a white man whose very existence opposed their way of life.

It is a great loss to our American history that John S. Smith died without having had a personal account of his life placed on paper. Lost forever is a lifetime of adventures in the wilderness of Western America; of happy, lazy days among the tribes; of exciting hunts upon the plains; of long, painful rides through summer heat and winter snows; of trades among the Cheyenne and pensive smokes with the old chiefs; of lonely fur-trapping excursions; of danger and conflict with hostile bands of warriors; of early day forts in remote corners of the wilderness; of great open ranges, cool prairie streams, and gleaming mountains in the far distance; of Indian warfare and throbbing dances through the night; of somber councils between red and white men; and interesting excursions to the East—all intermingled with the persistent dissolution of the old life as it was swept under by the undeniable tide of the white man's civilization.

John S. Smith was a vanguard figure in the historical drama of the American West, a man upon whom circumstances thrust a fateful calling. As the Cheyenne warrior was fitted to a life on the Plains, so Smith was fitted to this time and place of history. It was a life role which only he could have played.

No stone marks his grave near the banks of the North Canadian River just north of present El Reno, Oklahoma. About him were buried old friends from the Cheyenne and Arapaho tribes, perhaps keeping him company around the lodge fires of some eternal life beyond. For surely if old Blackfoot Smith found Heaven, it must be a place of open prairie, clear-running streams, and purple peaks against the far vistas of a blue sky.

1

Into the Wilderness

*. . . he left his employer, a tailor, and ran off from St. Louis,
with a party of traders for the mountains; and so enamored
was he with the desultory and exciting life, that he chose
rather to set cross-legged smoking the long Indian pipe, than
to cross his legs on his master's board. . .* Lewis Garrard[1]

By the year 1830 the North American continent was
not yet even half explored. The young nation of the
United States, only fifty-four years in existence and still
shaping itself in this new world of the Americas, had
barely reached the Mississippi River, on whose west bank
the settlement of St. Louis had been sired in 1764 by the
Frenchman Laclede. From here cadres of fur company
traders and hunters pushed off on long voyages up the
Missouri River, to the Green River country, and sometimes to the far shores of the Pacific. Trading caravans
with their ox-drawn wagons rattled southwestward down
the newly opened Santa Fe Trail to trade with the Mexicans at Taos and Santa Fe, returning months later with
wealths of fur, specie, and mules. Steamboats, their twin
stacks belching smoke and their paddle wheels churning a
froth behind, worked their way cautiously up and down
the great Mississippi River.

[1] Lewis H. Garrard, *Wah-to-Yah and the Taos Trail, The Southwest Historical
Series,* VI, ed. by Ralph Bieber (Glendale, Calif: The Arthur H. Clark Co.) 115.

From St. Louis had gone Lewis and Clark on their transcontinental exploration to the Pacific Northwest in 1804; Zebulon Pike, to explore the Southwest in 1807; Major Stephen Long, leading his small party up the Platte River to the Rocky Mountains in 1820; General Atkinson, who cordelled his flotilla of keelboats up the Missouri in 1825, signing peace treaties with the wild tribes along the river and firing his cannons and rockets to impress them with the strength of the whites; and a host of stalwart men whose deeds and names are stamped indelibly on the history of Western America: Jedediah Smith, Kit Carson, William Bent, James Bridger, William Ashley, Tom Fitzpatrick, William and Milton Sublette, and a legion of others.

Newspapers of the day printed accounts of Major Riley's escort of a wagon train as far south as the Arkansas River, then marking the boundary of Mexico; of General Ashley's fur-hunting expeditions in the western mountain regions; and of Governor William Clark's peace-making ventures with the northern tribes at Prairie-du-Chien. Daily men arrived in St. Louis to tell of hardships on the trail, of never-ending plains and trackless mountains, of Indian attacks and scalpings, of dangers from Yankee-hating Spanish patrols. They told also of buffalo herds that blackened the prairies, of the horses and robes to be traded from the friendlier tribes, and of the inexhaustible supply of furs and pelts to be taken from the virgin rivers of the western wilderness.

St. Louis, truly, was the gateway to the West. The settlement lay beneath a bluff on the Mississippi's west bank just below the mouth of the Missouri. Laclede had named his trading post in honor of Louis XV of France, and, though it was established on what was then Spanish soil and so remained for nearly forty years, its temperament and character was determined by the easy-living French Creoles who comprised its main population. In 1804, under terms of the Louisiana Purchase with Napoleon, a poignant ceremony was conducted at St. Louis wherein the Spanish flag was lowered, the French flag was raised, symbolic of the territory's transfer to France, and allowed to float over St. Louis for twenty-four hours on request of the French-blooded citizens. Then it was lowered and the Stars and Stripes was hoisted against the blue Missouri sky.

In 1815 a flood of Anglo-American immigration began pouring in upon the town, overrunning the settlement, causing many of the wealthier French to withdraw to areas outside the city. After 1817, when the first steamboat moored at the St. Louis levee, the frontier town began a rapid growth as a transportation center, and by 1830 its docks were lined with the cargo-laden paddlewheelers as well as keelboats and barges. St. Louis quickly developed as a trading center, particularly for the fur trade, and her streets began to stretch away from the river and up the limestone bluff onto the plateau leading beyond to the rolling, timbered land which marked the beginning of the wilderness.

Daniel Webster, a visitor to the town during the 1830's recounted the long, narrow streets of St. Louis, lined with fragile-looking tenement houses and populated with "long-legged, long-haired lanky backwoodsmen of Illinois; the stern, iron visage of the engagé of the American Fur Company; the dark, flashing eye and swarthy cheek of the French villager; the heavy form, astute, stolid features of German; the savage garb and reckless bearing of Mississippi boatman; and the lofty, dignified figure of Osage chiefs."[2]

---

[2] Washington D.C. *Daily National Intelligencer,* June 26, 1837.

Describing St. Louis during the same period, Washington Irving noted the mixture of French and American character. He told of the billiard room where the sounds of cue and billiard ball could be heard from morning until night, the French marketplace where a strange mixture of French and English was spoken, the rackety old gambling house of the town, and the French women in their native dress quarreling in the streets. Irving wrote, too, of being a guest in the plantation home of Governor Clark, the William Clark who over twenty-five years before had embarked from this same St. Louis with Captain Meriwether Lewis upon the first great exploring expedition of the American West. York, the famous black servant to Clark who had also made the historic voyage, was to be seen driving the Governor's carriage about.[3]

Thus by 1830 St. Louis had become a thriving center of commerce and the emporium for the western operation of the fur trade. It was this year that a young American named John Simpson Smith first went from the city to begin a long, eventful, and colorful life in the wilderness of the American West. His was an American odyssey which would last for over four decades, encompass virtually all of the Central Plains and Rocky Mountain regions, and involve such adventures as few men have ever known. But even beyond the adventure, Smith's career in the West was destined to have great effect upon the course of events during the crucial years that saw the domination of the West wrested from the Indian by the white man. Smith's role in this great historical epoch was a significant one.

John Smith—an altogether appropriate name to be cast in such a role. A name so typically American, yet already

---

[3] Washington Irving, *A Tour of the Prairies* (Oklahoma City: Harlow Publishing Corp., 1955), pp. xvi–xvii.

made famous by the renowned captain of Jamestown. The annals of the West list many men with the name of John Smith, some of them honestly titled, but for many it was a convenient cover for identities prior to their coming West. Certainly no name was more honorably known to the West than Smith. It was the daring western explorer, the God-fearing Jedediah Smith, who had blazed the first trails to Oregon, California, the Salt Lake region, and many other places where he had been among the first white men to gaze in awe upon the mysterious beauties of a land where civilized beings had never before trod.

John Simpson Smith had been carried to St. Louis as a boy by the tide of Anglo-American migration from the Middle Atlantic regions. Born at Frankfort, Kentucky, in 1810, he was twenty years of age and serving as a tailor's apprentice in 1830.[4] Such apprenticeships were legally binding contracts which placed the apprentice in complete servitude to his master, who often demanded excessively long hours of toil and provided little reward other than board and keep. Thus it was not at all surprising that the youthful Smith, hearing the exuberant tales of trappers and traders who crowded the saloons of St. Louis and seeing the rich loads of pelts and furs they brought with them, should look to the western wilderness for his freedom.

The early years of John Smith's life can be traced only by sparse clues placed in reference to known events. Since he had neither finances nor experience in the trade, it seems probable that he must have hired on with one of the major fur companies then operating out of St. Louis. The records account for several such trader groups leav-

---

[4] *Report of the Joint Special Committee Appointed Under Resolution of March 3, 1865*, "Condition of Indian Tribes," 39 cong., 2 sess., *Senate Report No. 156*, 41. Hereafter cited as *The Chivington Massacre.*

ing the city in 1830, the year that Smith states that he went West. In February a party under Fontenelle, Drips, and Joseph Robidoux left for the Green River country, reaching it in June.[5] The party's chronicler, Warren A. Ferris, does not mention any John Smith, though this may simply mean that Smith was not important enough for notice then.

William Sublette also led a large band of eighty-one trappers with ten mule-drawn wagons and twelve head of cattle to the Wind River rendezvous of 1830, bringing the first wheeled traffic on what came to be known as the Oregon Trail. It was at this rendezvous that Jedediah Smith, David Jackson, and William Sublette sold their mountain fur interests to five of their brigade leaders: Thomas Fitzpatrick, James Bridger, Milton Sublette, Henry Fraeb, and Jean Baptiste Gervais. This partnership operated out of St. Louis as the Rocky Mountain Fur Company.[6]

A band of some eighty men under Fitzpatrick, Milton Sublette, and Bridger left the rendezvous of August 1830, and penetrated the territory of the antagonistic Blackfoot Indians. John Smith's acquaintance with Fitzpatrick and his known association with the Blackfeet, point to the faint possibility that he may have been a member of this group. However, the Rocky Mountain group was in constant conflict with the Blackfeet, offering little chance for Smith to learn the Blackfoot language as he is known to have accomplished.

Evidence indicates that it may well have been the American Fur Company, whose Western Department had only recently been established in St. Louis under Ken-

---

[5] Warren A. Ferris, *Life in the Rocky Mountains*, Paul C. Phillips, ed. (Denver: The Old West Publishing Co., 1940), xli.

[6] Hiram Martin Chittenden, *The American Fur Trade of the Far West* (Stanford, Calif.: Academic Reprints, 1954), 291–92.

neth MacKenzie, with which John Smith first went west. MacKenzie, an aristocratic Scotsman of high ambition and energy, had been assigned the chore of opening to trade the Blackfoot country of present Montana.

The Blackfeet were American haters. Some said the Canadian fur companies to the north were largely to blame for encouraging the tribe's warriors to take Yankee scalps wherever and whenever they got the chance. This was no doubt the case, but the Blackfeet remembered that Captain Lewis had killed a Blackfoot when the American exploring expedition passed through their country in 1806. And they knew that John Colter, who had been with Lewis and Clark and later became a fur trapper, had fought against them with their hereditary enemies, the Crows.

Whatever the reason, the Blackfeet were violently determined to protect their fur-rich lands from encroachment by the American trappers and hunters. They rode the vast high plains and mountain regions of present Montana in large parties, well armed with British guns. The Americans might claim to have purchased this country from the French, but it was the Blackfoot warrior who ruled on the Marias, the Mussellshell, and the Yellowstone.

In 1807 when Manuel Lisa, Pierre Chouteau, and Colter began building a fort at the mouth of the Bighorn River, the Blackfoot warriors struck furiously, killing five of the trappers and making away with virtually all of their horses, guns, traps, and furs. Each year twenty or more men lost their lives and scalps to the Blackfeet. The tribe became so feared that in 1811 the Overland Astorians, traveling up the Missouri by boat toward Oregon, quit the river and bypassed the Blackfoot range on horseback rather than take the risk.

When Ashley and Henry attempted to work the Upper Missouri in the 1820's, they were driven out with severe losses. And in 1830 the large band of Americans under Fitzpatrick, Bridger, and Milton Sublette penetrated the region only because their large numbers discouraged open attack. Even they were forced to keep moving quickly on and out of the region.

Still the Blackfoot country was unquestionably the richest in furs of any in the American West, and the fur companies all yearned for a chance to exploit it. MacKenzie, like the other fur traders, knew the immense fur wealth controlled by the Blackfeet and was determined to be the first to develop a trade there.

While visiting his company's newly established Fort Union (1828) at the mouth of the Yellowstone River in the fall of 1830, MacKenzie came across an old Canadian trapper named Jacob Berger, who had spent over twenty years in the fur business to the north, knew the Blackfoot tongue, and was acquainted with some of their chiefs. MacKenzie persuaded the old trapper to lead a small party into Blackfoot country in an attempt to convince the tribe to open trade negotiations.[7]

Taking a dog sled loaded with gifts, the little group of four men, all French Canadians, headed westward from Fort Union along the Missouri River toward the Blackfoot country. It took them four weeks to reach the mouth of the Marias and move up the river a ways before they finally encountered a party of Piegans, a branch of the Blackfoot tribe, who led them to their main camp on the Sun River. Here they were hospitably received, but only because of Berger's acquaintance with some of the chiefs.

---

[7] Charles Larpenteur, *Forty Years a Fur Trader on the Upper Missouri* (Chicago: The Lakeside Press, 1933) vol. I, 109–15. Ferris, XCIV.

Berger distributed the gifts and was invited to remain with the Indians for a time. During this stay he talked the Blackfeet into taking a large party back to Fort Union to visit MacKenzie. After a long and hazardous journey, during which the Indians became suspicious and threatened the lives of the white men, they reached Fort Union, where MacKenzie entertained them lavishly. He finally secured their permission to send a clerk and four or five men into their country as traders, though the Indians were still violently against any hunters or trappers.

MacKenzie also signed a treaty with the Blackfeet, agreeing to build them a fort in their own country. In the fall of 1831 he sent a party of men under James Kipp, their keelboat loaded with trade goods, to the Marias River where in October they began building a fort for the Indians called Fort Piegan.[8]

Just what role John Smith may have played in this is not clear. Garrard, who knew Smith well, is precise in stating that Smith spent that first winter of 1830 with the Blackfeet.[9] This, plus the fact that Smith could speak the Blackfoot tongue and, because of it, was known to the Cheyennes as "Blackfoot" Smith, is evidence that he might well have been among the builders of Fort Piegan, which was burned by the Indians after being vacated by Kipp's party in the spring of 1831. D. D. Mitchell, an acquaintance of John Smith in later life, returned in the spring of 1832 and constructed Fort MacKenzie near the mouth of the Marias.

According to Garrard, Smith spent only one winter with the Blackfeet, finding that living among the hot-tempered, young braves of the tribe was precarious, indeed, for an American. Chiefs often had only limited con-

[8] Chittenden, 330–37. [9] Garrard, 115.

trol over their warriors to whom white scalps were a real prize. Undoubtedly, Smith found that the murderous looks cast his way by the bucks made his skin crawl and, as Garrard put it, ". . . . running too great a risk of 'losing his hair' (scalp) at the hands of the impetuous, *coup*-anxious braves, he sojourned awhile with the more friendly Sioux . . . ."[10]

It is quite possible, too, that Smith found working under MacKenzie not altogether to his liking. Though reputed to be far and away the most able trader in the business, this man who was related to the famous Canadian explorer, Alexander MacKenzie, was a virtual despot. His intolerance for error and his lack of compassion for his men were legend in the trade. One story concerning him told how he once offered to turn over an employee to a group of angry Indians who wished to revenge themselves for the death of a tribal member. Another reported that following a fight between a party of his men and some Indians, he asked how many horses had been killed. Upon learning that only the men had escaped, he replied in effect, "Damn the men! If the horses had been saved it would have amounted to something!"

It is doubtful that a man such as Smith, who had just escaped the binding and thankless servitude of one master, would have remained longer than necessary with another. The West of the 1830s offered something much better—virtually unlimited freedom for the man who had the courage to win it.

Based upon accounts of Smith's life during this period provided by old mountain men such as Sol Silver,[11] the young Kentuckian soon saw the futility of letting others make most of the profit from the hard and dangerous

---

[10] *Ibid.*

[11] Stanley Vestal, *Mountain Men* (Boston: Houghton Mifflin Co., 1937), 158.

efforts of fur trapping or losing an entire season's work, as
did many trappers, during the wild orgies of drinking and
gambling at the annual rendezvous. So, instead, he cached
most of his furs and pelts for the winter with the idea of
boating them down the Missouri to market in the spring.

As he had learned to do from the Indian tribes along the
river, he built himself a willow framework shaped like a
tub, stretched a buffalo robe tightly over the craft, tying
his robes to the framework, and set float with the current
toward St. Louis. But the boat soon hit a snag in the river
above Fort MacKenzie, capsizing and dunking Smith in
the cold water. Though he saved his furs and guns, he was
thoroughly chilled and dared not build a fire since he was
still in Blackfoot country. By morning a raging toothache
and neuralgic attack had him in severe pain.

In desperation Smith loaded his goods back into the
boat and headed to Fort MacKenzie. Arriving there early
one morning, he took a few beaverskins from his packs,
pounded on the gate until a sleepy clerk appeared, and
purchased a jug of liquor and a bottle of laudanum, a
tincture of opium used on the river as a pain reliever. A
few swigs of both soon put him in good shape to continue
on his way. The pain gone and the sun now making him
warm and comfortable in the bullboat, Smith once again
spun and bounced with the sweeping tide of the river
toward Missouri.

In his drowsy comfort, however, Smith did not notice
that five Blackfoot braves had spotted him and were heading him off at a bend of the winding river. The current
swept him close to the bank and under the control of their
guns so that he was forced to comply with their signals for
him to come ashore.

There the Blackfeet met him. They took his hands and
dragged him from the boat, afterward helping themselves to all

his property. Then they slit the bullboat with their knives and sent it drifting away, sinking as it went. They led Smith up the bank and out upon the prairie.

Up there the wind was chill and disagreeable. Herding Smith before them, the five warriors rode their ponies to a sheltered spot not far off, where they dismounted and built a fire to roast the meat they had found in the bullboat. Smith saw they were going to eat first—and probably murder him after. Meanwhile they had found the alcohol; it made Smith laugh to see them try to swallow the raw spirit. But hoping to get them all drunk, he showed them how to dilute it with water, so that they could get it down.

By that time his dose of laudanum had lost its power, and he took another dose from the bottle in his pocket. This aroused the curiosity of his captors; they tried to take the bottle from him. Smith would not let them have it. He would rather have lost his scalp than that bottle. He told them it was dangerous "medicine." But he offered to give each a little . . . He gave each one a dose to knock him out. When the drug took effect, one after another fell asleep. Smith relaxed. He had got the best of them.

Smith helped himself to their powder and lead and buffalo robes, cleaned and reloaded his guns, picked a fast horse to ride, and filled his saddlebags with meat. He broke all the bows and arrows, threw them on the fire, and tossed all the guns and knives into the creek. Then he rounded up the ponies and was ready to start . . .

However, just as he was ready to start, two more Blackfeet rode over the hill. Smith did not shoot . . . He let them come up to the campfire. When they saw the burning bows and their friends lying around as if dead, one of them drew a bead on Smith. But Smith had the first shot and dropped him. The second Injun tried to ride away, but Smith shot his horse and the animal bucked the Blackfoot off on his head. Before he could throw off his daze, Smith was on him . . . He got the Injun down, stabbed him . . .

Smith suddenly understood how the Injun fighters felt. He scalped every one of those Blackfeet—seven of them—taking care to leave the white shells, the brass wire, and other trinkets tied to their hair.

Smith wrapped the scalps in a piece of buffalo hide, . . .
rounded up his horses, swam them across the river . . . and
struck out for Crow country to the southeast. The laudanum so
dulled his aches and pains that he was able to ride day and night
as long as the horse could travel. On the Yellowstone he fell in
with a party of trappers traveling with some friendly Sioux.
Smith gave each of the Sioux a horse from his band—the animals
were pretty well worn down by that time—and so made himself
welcome in their camps.[12]

Though Smith's trail through the West during his early
years is dim, indeed, there are some clues which indicate
his possible activities. He is cited in Wyoming historical
records as being a pioneer of that state as early as 1832.[13]
This appears to be altogether possible and likely, for this
region was a favorite trapping and hunting ground for the
fur traders from the very beginning. John Colter had first
entered the northwestern corner in 1807, and after 1812
the mountain men became active along the Wyoming
rivers where the beaver and other game were abundant.

It could have been that the ex-tailor's apprentice was
the "Smith" with a company of fur traders, led by Gantt
and Blackwell, which was on the Platte in Wyoming during the summer of 1832.[14]

Zenas Leonard, a member of the party who later wrote
an account of his travels, tells how he hunted and trapped
on the Platte and its tributaries with a man named Smith
and how on one occasion Smith and another comrade
helped save him from a grizzly bear. This Smith was also
with Leonard's party, which joined up with Fitzpatrick

[12] Ann W. Hafen, "John Simpson Smith," *Mountain Men and the Fur Trade*,
LeRoy R. Hafen, ed. (Glendale, Calif: The Arthur H. Clark Co., 1968), vol. v, 327–29,
quoting from Vestal, *Mountain Men*, 178–81.

[13] *Annals of Wyoming*, vol. 6, nos. 1–2 (July–October, 1929), 240.

[14] Zenas Leonard, *Narrative of the Adventures of Zenas Leonard* (Ann Arbor:
University Microfilms, Inc., 1966), 12–13, 22.

that summer and took part in the famous Battle of Pierre's Hole against the Blackfeet following the rendezvous there in July, 1832. By Leonard's account, Smith was wounded in the foot during an attempt to advance on the Blackfoot fortification. Leonard states that he carried Smith to safety during the battle, but this is the last mention of the man in Leonard's narrative, and no further clue to his identity is provided.

Whether or not this may have been John Simpson Smith is pure speculation. Garrard places him in Sioux country—which Wyoming was—during this period, while Smith himself testified to a Congressional committee that prior to his joining the Cheyennes in 1838 he "was in the country as a trapper and a hunter."[15] Accordingly, it is possible for Smith to have been among the 400 white men which Leonard estimated to be present at the 1832 rendezvous at Pierre's Hole: over a hundred men of the Rocky Mountain Fur Company under Fitzpatrick, including the Gantt and Blackwell men; a party of ninety-some under Vanderburgh and Drips of the American Fur Company; Nathaniel Wyeth's party of eighteen raw Bostonians; William Sublette with about sixty men; plus a large number of free trappers whose tents were scattered among those of the Flathead and Nez Percé bands at the rendezvous.

Following the meeting, Milton Sublette and Gervais led a band of trappers to the southwest while William Sublette took a large pack train back to St. Louis. Wyeth's party, joined by a small group of free trappers, headed for Jackson's Hole where they were attacked by Blackfeet and lost three men. Fitzpatrick and Bridger took off for

---

[15] "Massacre of Cheyenne Indians," *Report of the Joint Committee on the Conduct of the War*, 38 Cong., 2 sess., Senate Report No. 142, 11. Hereafter cited as *Massacre of Cheyenne Indians*.

the headwaters of the Missouri, hoping to elude Vanderburgh and Drips, who were dogging them to find good
hunting areas. Fraeb returned to the head of the Grand
River in the Colorado mountains.

When Fitzpatrick and Bridger found Vanderburgh and
Drips still on their trail, they plunged into the heart of
Blackfoot country, luring their greenhorn rivals into the
waiting arms of the Indians who attacked the party, killed
Vanderburgh, and threw his bones into the river. It was
during this venture into Blackfoot country that Bridger
was hit twice by arrows, carrying one of the iron arrowheads in his back for nearly three years.[16]

If Garrard is correct that John Smith remained essentially in Sioux country, it is a distinct likelihood that he
was in the vicinity when William Sublette and thirteen
men constructed Fort William at the confluence of the
North Platte and Laramie rivers in June of 1834. Here
Sublette conducted trading operations with the Sioux and
Cheyenne until 1835, at which time he sold the post to
Fitzpatrick, Milton Sublette, and Bridger, who soon
turned it over to the American Fur Company.

DeB. Randolph Keim, *New York Herald* reporter who
knew Smith in 1868, has the ex-tailor's apprentice covering an even wider area during this period: "Being of a
roving and adventurous disposition, he set out for the
great and unexplored West. As a trapper he traversed the
vast region west of the Mississippi, and finally found himself on the Pacific slope of the Rocky Mountains. Here he
passed seven years, then he returned east of the Rocky
Mountains."[17]

In the absence of more precise records of Smith during
the 1830–1838 period, it is possible still to speculate on

[16] Chittenden, 330–37.   [17] *New York Herald*, Dec. 12, 1868.

his activities which had made him a seasoned frontiersman and Indian trader by the time that Garrard met him
in 1846. Though most of his adventures during this time,
like so many of the unrecorded events of the early West,
are lost to history forever, it is certain that Smith hunted
and trapped the rivers and streams of the Northern Plains
and Rockies, that he lived among the Indians in their
buffalo skin lodges, subsisted on their diets, joined in their
hunts, rode in and out of the early forts with his pack
horses laden with furs, and roamed about the West in full
pleasure of the great freedom he now possessed.

It seems evident that he lived the existence of a free
trapper and a mountain man, that highly independent
breed of western fur man who captured and sold on his
own without attachment or subservience to any of the
major fur companies. These men were bound to no one
except themselves and generally moved in small groups
wherever they wished to go. Regarded as the boldest and
most adventurous of all the fur traders, they were fierce of
spirit and contemptuous of civilization. Many of them
adopted the Indian's ways, took up Indian wives, spoke a
"mountain man" language all their own, dressed in frilled
buckskins, and were fond of fancy geegaws with which
they ornamented their horses and themselves. By and
large, they had the reputation as expert marksmen and
hard fighters, and Indians of all tribes soon learned to
leave them alone except when they were badly outnum-
bered.

A tradition of comradeship was strong among them,
and as a class of men they enjoyed sport to excess. Their
rendezvous were virtual orgies of gambling, drinking,
story telling, and horse racing. The Reverend Samuel
Parker, present at the rendezvous of 1835 on the Green
River, tells how Dr. Whitman removed the Blackfoot ar-

row which had been in the back of Jim Bridger for three
years, how Kit Carson accepted the challenge of a camp
bully to a duel on horseback and shattered the man's arm
with a bullet, how the irreverent traders sold the Indians a
pack of cards at high prices, telling them the pack was the
Bible and that if they refused to give the white men wives,
God would be angry and punish them.[18] The odds are
good that John Smith, who knew both Bridger and Carson
well, was there at the rendezvous of 1835.

Nothing was so important to the free trapper as his
personal freedom, which the rugged life in the wilderness
alone could provide, and it was this group of men which
produced some of the greatest characters of the fur trading era in America. Garrard's description of John Smith so
perfectly fits the mold of the free trapper that there can
be little doubt that the Kentuckian indulged in such an
existence during the 1830–1838 period.

The free trapper quickly developed a language all his
own, created out of corrupted English, French, Spanish,
and smatterings of the many Indian dialects which he
encountered. Like the geegaws on his gear and the frills
on his buckskins, much of his conversation was put-on for
the sake of show and self-identity, and most mountain
men, Smith included, could turn it on or off as they chose.

A mountain man often referred to himself as "this
chil'," to a friend as an "old coon" or "old hoss." Buffalo
were "buffler" and lean buffalo meat dried as jerky was
known as "poor bull." When someone was killed or died,
he was said to have "gone under" and many a time someone came "mighty nigh close to losing 'is hair." "Wagh!"
or "By beaver!" were favorite expressions, and a real
mountain man would "keep his eye skinned" and put up

---

[18] Rev. Samuel Parker, *Journal of an Exploring Tour Beyond the Rocky Mountains* (Ithaca, New York: Mack, Andrees and Woodruff, Printers; 1840), 79–84.

with but little "fofaraw" from a "greenhorn." Though
Garrard and others are undoubtedly correct in quoting
John Smith as using the mountain man modes of expression, recorded testimony by Smith in a number of instances is in plain and simple English. The same is true
of James Beckwourth, the mulatto mountain man.

In the spring of the year, Smith and the other free
traders would "make up their packs" and head for a rendezvous, for one of the trading posts, or perhaps downriver for the frontier Missouri settlements to sell their
winter's haul and to enjoy a period of celebration and
story telling before re-outfitting for a return to the trapping grounds. Those with Indian wives usually returned to
the tribe and took part in their summer and fall hunts.
Some of them hung around the forts, some hired out as
guides for western immigration, and some hiked off on
exploratory jaunts to places they had heard tell about and
not yet seen.

Ironically, it was the clothing trade which reached into
the wilderness during the 1830's and drastically affected
the way of life for the ex-tailor's apprentice and the other
free traders. The fur companies and the men who worked
in the fur trade made their profits largely from the sale of
beaver skins which were used to make clothing, particularly the high-topped beaver headgear worn by fashionable folks in Europe and the Eastern United States. The
introduction of the silk hat during the 1830s greatly diminished the demand for beaver pelts, which came
mainly from the high plains of the Rocky Mountains.
Thus by 1838, the trade in beaver skins had fallen off
badly, and the men who had once set the beaver trap now
began to look to the great buffalo herds and to trade with
the Indian tribes of the middle plains for a livelihood.

Garrard states that Smith ". . . wended his way, while pursuing the trail of a horse-stealing band of Arapahoes, to the headwaters of the Arkansas: and, in the quiet nooks and warm savannas of the Bayou Salade [South Park] he took up his abode and a squaw, with the Cheyennes . . ."[19] But there can be little doubt that the drop off in the beaver trade was a prime factor for his move. Smith himself indicated that his acquaintance with the Cheyennes came as a result of his trading activities with Bent and St. Vrain, which hints that he came south for reason of employment rather than by happenstance. He was by no means alone. When the Rocky Mountain trapping brigades began breaking up in 1838, Kit Carson also returned south to Bent's Fort, where he had been employed in the early thirties.

Smith's trapping and hunting period ended and his long association with Bent's Fort and the Cheyenne Indians began in 1838. Behind him were eight years of experience in the wilderness, and he was now a seasoned frontiersman. Ahead of him lay a new career as an Indian trader.

---

[19] Garrard, 115. Smith stated in 1865 that "Since I went there I have resided with the Indians off and on every year; I have generally been employed as a United States interpreter; prior to that I was a trader in that country for St. Vrain & Co., and in that way I first learned the Cheyenne language." *The Chivington Massacre*, 43.

BENT'S FORT

Bent's Fort on the Arkansas, as drawn by Lt. Abert in 1845. John Simpson Smith was a fur trader for many years at the fort.

Courtesy, Denver Public Library Western Collection

2

Bent's Fort Days

He became such an adept in the knowledge of Cheyenne tongue and such a favorite with the tribe that his services as trader were now quite invaluable to his employers. Possessed of a retentive memory, he still spoke the dialects of the three nations just named [Blackfoot, Sioux, and Cheyenne]; and in addition, French like a native, Spanish very well; his mother tongue. Though subject to privations of a severe nature, he thought it Better to reign in hell than serve in heaven, *and nothing could persuade him to lead a different life. . .*

Lewis Garrard[1]

John Smith was twenty-eight years of age when he moved to the Arkansas River to become a Bent's Fort trader. Located on the north bank of the Arkansas River in present Colorado, Bent's Fort stood as the solitary outpost of civilization between Missouri and New Mexico. Founded by the Bent and St. Vrain Company during the early 1830s, the fort was surrounded by the hunting ranges of the wild Plains tribes.

When Thomas Farnham visited the fort in 1839, he saw it almost as "an old baronial castle that has withstood the wars and desolations of centuries." Doctor Wislizenus, visiting the same year, described how the courtyard was filled with barnyard fowl, while "in addition they have

---

[1] Garrard, *Wah-to-Yah*, 115–16.

cattle, sheep and goats, and three buffalo calves that peacefully graze with the rest of the herd."[2]

Despite the potential danger presented by the Indians, the fort was often surrounded by Indian encampments without once undergoing an attack other than upon its horse herds. Farnham related how the big gates would be swung open in the morning to allow the long-braided, curious-faced Indians to slide in and out. He told, too, of the busy clerks and traders, of patrols walking the battlements with their loaded muskets, of guards in the bastion standing by the cannonades with lighted matches. At night the Indians filled the air with their singing and dancing.

Farnham watched the traders, clad in buckskin hunting shirts and leggins with long fringes on the outer seams, ride in and out of the fort and, in moments of leisure, sit cross-legged in the shade smoking the long-stemmed stone Indian pipe. He noted their leathery, weather-lined faces and listened to their stories of adventures or discussions of where the buffalo were and which Indian bands were presently hostile.[3] Undoubtedly Smith was among them, though Farnham does not mention him by name.

It was in this setting that John Smith began his long and intimate association with the Cheyenne Indians. More than capable of competing with the men of the tribe in the skills of tracking and hunting, he also quickly learned the Cheyenne tongue, which gave him an important position with the tribe as an interpreter and mediator with the whites. Furthermore, as trader with the Cheyennes he

---

[2] F.A. Wislizenus, *A Journey to the Rocky Mountains in the Year 1839*, Translated from the German (St. Louis: Missouri Historical Society, 1912), 141.

[3] Thomas J. Farnham, *Travels in the Great Western Prairie, the Anahuac and Rocky Mountains, and in Oregon Territory* (New York: Greeley & McElrath, 1843), 37–40.

performed a service much desired by the Indians. The tribe had already developed a taste for many of the white man's goods such as sugar, coffee, tobacco, and so forth, plus a dependency on the trade for such items as gunpowder, lead balls, percussion caps, cloth, decorative beads, and many other things for which they willingly bargained their furs and extra horses. They had long yearned to have a white trader among them, as Captain Bell of the Long expedition indicated when his group met some Cheyennes on the Arkansas in 1820. Though Bell described the Cheyennes as the "most dreaded and feared of all other nations," the white men were cordially treated and invited to send traders among them.[4]

Smith's arrival among the Cheyennes on the Arkansas coincided with the great victory by them and the Arapahoes over the Kiowas and Comanches at Wolf Creek in present northwestern Oklahoma. It was this success that won the two tribes the right to range south of the river without fear of attack by the southern bands. Smith was very likely present when the four warring tribes held their great peace council below Bent's Fort in 1840, exchanged gifts, danced, celebrated, and made their historic peace agreement.

Smith took up a lodge and a squaw with the Cheyennes, living with them as a trader during the winter seasons and traveling with them much of the summer when the trade was off, hunting the buffalo and depending on it for an existence the same as the Cheyennes. His Cheyenne wife was a widow who already had a full-blood son, likely of some warrior who had been killed in battle. Smith's first-

---

[4] Harlin M. Fuller and LeRoy R. Hafen, eds., *The Journal of Captain John R. Bell, Official Journalist for the Stephen H. Long Expedition to the Rocky Mountains, 1820,* vol. VI of *The Far West and the Rockies Historical Series, 1820–1875* (Glendale, Calif: The Arthur H. Clark Co., 1957), 194.

born was a son named John—Garrard humorously noted that Smith was probably afraid the name "John Smith" would go out of use. The boy, who was called Jack, appears to have been born around 1842.

As a trader, Smith was accorded a place of high esteem by the Cheyennes, virtually that of a chief, and he found the new life very much to his liking. Smith's part in the trade and his position with the Cheyennes are described in detail by Garrard:

> The New Mexicans often came in small parties to his Indian village; their mules packed with dried pumpkin, corn, etc., to trade for robes & meat; and Smith, who knew his power, exacted tribute which was always paid. One time, however, refusing, Smith harangued the village, and calling the young men together, they resolutely proceeded to the party of cowering Mexicans; and emptying every sack on the ground, called the women and children to help themselves, which summons was obeyed with alacrity. The poor *pelados* left for El Valle de Taos poorer by far than when they came: uttering thanks to Heaven for the retention of their scalps. This and other aggravated cases so intimidated the New Mexicans and impressed them so deeply with a sense of Smith's potency that ever after his permission to trade was humbly craved by a special deputation of the parties, accompanied by peace offerings of corn, pumpkin, and *pinole*. Once as he was journeying by himself a day's ride from the village, he was met by forty or more corn traders; who instead of putting speedily out of the way such a bane to their prospects, gravely asked him if they could proceed; and offered him every third robe (a large percentage) to accompany and protect them, which he did. For the proceeds of his three days' protection he received more than two hundred dollars. Indeed he became so independent and so regardless of justice in his condescensions toward the *Carahos*, that the Governor of New Mexico offered five hundred dollars for him dead or alive; but so afraid were they of the Cheyennes, his capture was never attempted.[5]

---

[5] Garrard, *Wah-to-Yah*, 116.

As the principal Bent's Fort trader with the Cheyennes, Smith ranged with the tribe over their vast hunting grounds along the Arkansas and the South Platte. He was also involved in Bent's trading operations with the Comanches and Kiowas to the south in Texas and took part in the founding of the first Fort Adobe in the Texas Panhandle. The precise date of this is not clear. Bent and St. Vrain trading operations to the south were noted as early as 1835 when Colonel Henry Dodge and his dragoons visited the fort. George Bent, son of William Bent who claimed to have heard the story of Fort Adobe from both John Smith and Kit Carson, puts the date as prior to 1844.[6] It seems apparent that the founding of Fort Adobe took place after Smith joined the trading company in 1838 and before Kit Carson left Bent to guide Fremont in 1842.

Wishing to establish more permanent trading relations with the horse-rich Comanche and Kiowa tribes, William Bent dispatched some of his best men to the headwaters of the South Canadian River with trade goods to build a post there. This group included Smith, Carson, Murray, Maxwell, and Fisher, along with a cook and a herder.

The main purpose of the trade was not robes but horses. The fort was built of adobe, for trees were scarce in this rugged, gulley-slashed country of the Texas Pan-

---

[6] George Bird Grinnell, *The Fighting Cheyennes* (Norman, Okla: University of Oklahoma Press, 1958), 319–20. In August, 1843, Smith was back in the Fort Laramie vicinity where he was met by John C. Fremont's party westbound on a second expedition. Theodore Talbot mentions seeing Smith and Solomon Sublette there on August 5 and that Smith "frequently resides among the Indians and speaks at present purest Sheyenne," Theodore Talbot, *The Journals of Theodore Talbot* (Portland: Metropolitan Press 1931), 34. A letter from Fort Pierre in September of 1843 lists John Smith as being in the employ of Pratte, Cabrina & Co. "who could testify as to the sale of whiskey to the Sioux by traders at Fort Platte (Laramie)." Drips Papers, Missouri Historical Society, O. Sarpy to Major A. Drips.

handle, and trade was commenced. The Bent men did very well for a time, obtaining a large herd of horses and mules, which they corralled inside the fort at night.

But one day the inevitable happened, and an Indian raiding party struck, killing a Mexican herder and running off the entire herd except for two or three mules. There was no hope of remaining and recuperating their losses or even continuing to operate without horses to ride, and the traders had to abandon the fort.

Caching what they could not carry, the men loaded their remaining goods on the mules and started at night across the barren prairie for Bent's Fort on foot, suffering badly from cactus which penetrated their moccasins.

When daylight came, the group was discovered by a band of Indians, possibly Comanches, who made ready to attack. Murray, who was in command of the group, ordered the traders to scatter out. When one of the warriors attacked with a lance he was immediately dropped from his horse, and two more were killed by the deadly fire of this experienced band of plainsmen. The Indians finally withdrew.

When Colonel Stephen Watts Kearny's Army of the West passed Bent's Fort on its way to invade New Mexico in the summer of 1846, a young lieutenant, James W. Abert, was left behind ill with fever. During the months that followed, Abert proved himself an interested observer of frontier life. In his studies of the Indians and Indian language, he received invaluable help from John Smith.

> As my room was full of Cheyennes, I had the opportunity to obtain some knowledge of the genius and structure of their language. I found the English alphabet sufficient to represent all the sounds they utter, and at once set myself to work to con-

struct a vocabulary of their language. I had the assistance of one
of the best interpreters in the country.[7]

That he was referring to Smith can be of little doubt,
since on another occasion Abert wrote:

> During the day, one of the Indians brought me a specimen of
> the "astragalus" locoweed and told me that it was so poisonous
> as to kill any animal that might eat of it. Thinking it would be a
> good opportunity to learn the uses of the plants I had collected,
> and medical properties with which the experience of the Indi-
> ans invested them, I therefore produced my specimens, and
> with the assistance of Mr. Smith, who trades for the fort, and
> who speaks the Cheyenne language better, perhaps, than any
> other white person in the country, I made notes of everything
> that my red friends communicated.[8]

The stature which Smith held with the Indians is evidenced in a proposal which the officer tells of Cheyenne
chief Yellow Wolf making to the trader: "He [Yellow
Wolf] has proposed to the interpreter at Bent's fort, to
give him a number of mules, in the proportions of one
from every man in the tribe, if he would build them a
structure similar to Bent's fort, and instruct them to cultivate the ground, and to raise cattle."[9]

On the other hand, it may have been Smith to whom
George F. Ruxton referred when he wrote:

> Here congregate at certain seasons the merchants of the
> plains and mountains, with their stock of peltry. Chiefs of the
> Shian, the Kioway, and Arapaho, sit in solemn conclave with the
> head traders, and smoke the "calumet" over their real and imag-
> inary grievances. Now O-cun-no-whurst, the Yellow Wolf,
> grand chief of the Shian, complains of certain grave offences
> against the dignity of his nation! A trader from the "big lodge"
> (the fort) has been in his village, and before the trade was

---

[7] W. H. Emory, *Notes of a Military Reconnaissance, from Fort Leavenworth, in Missouri, to San Diego, in California*, 30 Cong., 1 sess., *House Executive Document No. 41*, 426.   [8] *Ibid.*, 425.   [9] *Ibid.*, 422.

opened, in laying the customary chief's gift "on the prairie" has not "opened his hand," but squeezed out his present "between his fingers" grudgingly and with too sparing measure. This was hard to bear, but the Yellow Wolf would say no more.[10]

In November of 1846, a wagon train passing by Bent's Fort dropped off another visitor, a frail, youthful Cincinnatian who was counting on a sojourn in the West to provide him with improved health and some interesting adventure. Lewis Garrard, who returned to the East the following year to write and publish his *Wah-to-Yah and the Taos Trail,* had the good fortune to meet and become friends with a man who could show him the country.

> On the evening of the 8th of November I started for the Indian village with John Smith. Yes! John Smith! the veritable John Smith! After leaving cities, towns, steamboats, and the civilized world, and traversing the almost boundless plains; here at the base of the Rocky Mountains, among buffalo, wild Indians, traders, and Spanish mules, have I found a John Smith.[11]

So impressed was Garrard with Smith that he decided to leave the security of the fort and venture forth into the Indian camps with the frontiersman. To the Easterner, Smith seemed almost like a feudal prince as he led his small caravan eastward from Bent's place along the Arkansas. Garrard rode at his side, while behind them followed Smith's Cheyenne squaw, a woman of about thirty, astride a high-pommeled Indian saddle. Over the saddle was blue cloth, beautifully worked with multicolored beads and with tin pellets that jangled from the fringed edges, which covered her horse from wethers to rump.[12]

Smith's half-blood son, Jack, still a baby at only three to four years of age, clung tightly to his mother, his complexion and features evidencing his Indian blood and his

---

[10] George Frederick Ruxton, *Life in the Far West* (Norman, Okla: University of Oklahoma Press, 1951), 180.

[11] Garrard, *Wah-to-Yah,* 95.   [12] *Ibid.,* 95–96.

grey eyes staring stoically out at all the world with baby-
ish curiosity. Small wonder that Garrard was much taken
with the child.

Smith's squaw had another ten-year-old son, a full-
blood, and he cantered along on his Indian pony. Behind
came Smith's wagon, four-mule drawn, driven by a Canadian Frenchman by the name of Pierre, hauling the bed-
ding, provisions, and the necessary goods for trading skins
and mules from the Indians.

Arriving at the Big Timbers, a famous camping place
for both whites and Indians, the Smith lodge was erected,
and "Blackfoot," as the Cheyennes called Smith, made
known his intentions of bartering. An Indian crier was at
once dispatched to inform the village:

> Throwing back the skin door of the lodge, he protruded his
> head and then his whole body, and uttered in a stentorian voice,
> something similar to the following, "*Hibbolo, Hibbolo! Po-ome,
> ho-o-o, nah wah-he, se-ne-mone, nah tah-ti-ve woh-pshe-
> o-nun, nah mok-ta-bo woh-pshe-o-nun, nah woh-pi woh-pshe-
> o-nun, nah mo-tah-ke, nah o-ne-ah-wokst;*" meaning in regular
> succession, that "Blackfoot (Smith), had come for mules; and all
> who wished to come and trade; that we had tobacco, blue blan-
> kets, black (deep blue) blankets, white blankets, knives, and
> beads."[13]

Garrard, who passed most of the winter of 1846–47 in
Smith's lodge, came to know the man probably as well as
anyone who wrote of him. The young visitor discovered
that while Smith was certainly a peculiar codger in many
respects, he was nonetheless endowed with special abili-
ties to adapt to circumstances and possessed such powers
of perception that he could quickly pick up a little knowledge of almost everything and then use it to his own
advantage.

Mountain men of the free trapper variety, Garrard

---

[13] *Ibid.,* 101.

came to realize, were a wonderment of contradictions, especially so John Smith: "Yet these aliens from society, these strangers to the refinements of civilized life who will tear off a bloody scalp with even grim smiles of satisfaction, are fine fellows, full of fun and often kind and obliging."[14] And he found John Smith to be a strange mixture "of goodness and evil, cleverness and meanness, caution and recklessness," as much a curiosity as any.[15]

Garrard gives a variety of interesting details which paint a vivid picture of Smith and his life among the Cheyennes. He tells of Smith's interest in news from the States and how the two of them discussed the Battle of New Orleans, wondering if there would be another war. He relates how they played backgammon in Smith's lodge, occasionally having to put it to one side to wait on an Indian customer who would often take an hour or more looking over a blanket and handling it before making a deal. He describes how they made winter camp on the trail, smoking their pipes around the campfire while a blizzard raged about them, comfortable at night in their warm buffalo robes with only their noses exposed to the weather. And in the cold dawn Smith would stir in his robes and mutter, "B'low zero, wah! Too cold! Darn breakfast, when a feller's fixed; I wouldn't git up for the fattest meat as runs on the peraira; t'aint often this buffler *is* comfortable, an' when he is, he knows it."[16]

Through Garrard's intimate account, Smith is shown downing an antelope with his first shot at 200 yards; cutting out pantaloons for the Easterner whose trousers had worn out; holding his temper despite his annoyance at being kept awake at night by the "infernal noise" of Indian dancers; generously dividing his scant meat supply

<hr />

[14] *Ibid.*, 114.   [15] *Ibid.*, 117.   [16] *Ibid.*, 160.

with a friend on the trail; and joshing Garrard when an Indian girl friend ran off with a buck. But always, when he was in the Cheyenne camp, Smith behaved with a special dignity befitting the high regard accorded him as a trader and important man by the Indians.

> I used to look at him with astonishment and wonder if he was not the devil incog. He & I often sang hymns, and a more sanctimonious, meek, at-peace-with-mankind look could nowhere be found than in his countenance; at other times he *sacré-ed* in French, *caraho-ed* in Spanish-Mexican, interpolated with *thunder strike you* in Cheyenne, or at others, he emphatically damned in American.[17]

As a vocalist, Smith was a fair hand, and he thoroughly enjoyed harmonizing with his guest. Together they would sing "The Days When We Went Gipsying," "The Mellow Horn," or perhaps "The Minstrel's Returned from the War." Their songfests amused the women and children, but the old Cheyenne warriors would shake their heads and decide that white men were truly fools. Generally, though, the duet would be invaded by the howling of the camp dogs, eventually "forcing us to acknowledge ourselves beaten in fair fight, and to withdraw, leaving them undisputed masters of the field . . ."[18]

During this stay with Smith and family, Garrard became attached to little Jack, who was also known by the Indian nickname of *Wo-pe-kon-ne*, meaning "White Eyes," and his formal Cheyenne name of *O-toz-vout-si*, meaning "Buck Deer." Though Jack could speak only Cheyenne and Garrard's communication with the little fellow was limited, he developed a fondness for the strange combination of lint-white hair that topped a Cheyenne-structured face and greyish eyes that shone forth from copperish skin.

---

[17] *Ibid.*, 117.   [18] *Ibid.*, 117–118.

Later, when it came time to part, the Cincinnatian realized that "Little Jack had contributed much to my happiness; for, although he could not talk American, the sight to me was an oasis in a desert. Among rough men and no kind words, Jack, at least, was not void of childish affection, and to amuse and talk to him, recalled home and cheerful retrospections."[19]

It was from Smith's Indian-style training of Jack that Garrard was to learn much about the harsh raising of Plains Indian children:

> . . . Jack took a crying fit one cold night, much to the annoyance of four or five chiefs who had come to our lodge to talk and smoke. In vain did the mother shake and scold him with the severest Cheyenne words until Smith, provoked beyond endurance, took the squalling youngster in hand; he "shu-ed" and shouted and swore, but Jack had gone too far to be easily pacified. He then sent for a bucket of water from the river and poured cupfull after cupfull on Jack, who stamped and screamed and bit, in his puny rage. Notwithstanding the icy stream slowly descended until the bucket was emptied, another was sent for, and again and again the cup was replenished and emptied on the blubbering youth. At last, exhausted with exertion and completely cooled down, he received the remaining water in silence, and with a few words of admonition was delivered over to his mother, in whose arms he stifled his sobs until his heartbreaking grief and cares were drowned in sleep.[20]

On another occasion, when Smith was camped on an Arkansas River sandbar near the mouth of Sand Creek, the boy took to another crying fit and resisted his mother's efforts to quiet him. After enduring this for half an hour, the impatient Smith dragged the child away from his mother, "who looked daggers askance at her unfeeling lord," and jammed Jack into the dray where he cried for two hours unheeded.[21]

---

[19] *Ibid.*, 339.   [20] *Ibid.*, 107–10.   [21] *Ibid.*, 135–36.

Garrard also gives several indications that Smith, like the Indian man-of-the-house, was a tyrannical husband who demanded much of his wife and tolerated very little error. On an occasion when Cheyenne chief Yellow Wolf was a visitor to Smith's lodge, the woman inadvertently let the kettle boil over on the lodge fire, the liquid raising a cloud of ash dust when it fell. Yellow Wolf immediately laid down his pipe, bent to the ground and covered his head with his robe for several moments. This, because of the Cheyenne superstition that the ember dust would cause a disease of the eye.

Such accidents often resulted in the lodge-poling of the squaw, and though Smith restrained himself in this instance, he did give his alarmed mate several menacing looks that reminded her of previous punishment which had been meted out for such an offense.[22]

Garrard was a keen observer and reporter, and his account of his visit presents an excellent picture of the Indian trader's life which Smith must have led for much of his stay in the West: the Indian foods (the Cheyennes were dog eaters), the raising of children, the Indian love of fun and sport, the ever-present discomfort of lice, and the dangers which existed on the wild frontier, not just for greenhorns like Garrard but even for experienced frontiersmen like Smith. One such occasion was the meeting with a bad-tempered Arapaho war party on the Arkansas that winter.

. . . Seeing a party approaching, Smith called my attention to it with—

"Look ahead! there's white men."

I gave a shout, at the same moment digging my spurs into the mule's side—"Hooray, we'll have meat and coffee to-night; but look! they wear Mexican hats."

---

[22] *Ibid.*, 175.

"So they do," replied he, after a scrutiny; "but they won't bother us, they know me too well to cut 'shine—John Smith's a name not to be grinned at by a darned carahoing 'palou'—Wagh! Indians, 'by beaver!'" hurriedly said he, changing his tone, "keep your eye skinned; I have left my gun in the wagon and have nothing but a knife."

I put on a fresh cap without changing its position, so as not to excite the attention of the coming party, though one gun was as nothing against thirty Arapahoes. We met them with as little show of trepidation as could be helped, and advancing to the foremost savage, offered our hands. The fellow took the proffered advance of amity with coldness, and stopped still. We dared not pass by, and asked him—

Ten-o-wast? "What is it you wish?"

He looked silently at us and again we chidingly asked in the Cheyenne tongue, "Ten-o-wast?"

Ni-hi-ni, ve-heo, mat-se-bo, e-se-vone Arapaho, answered he. The amount of his answer was that the "whiteman was bad, that he ran the buffalo out of the country, and starved the Arapaho."

Smith explained that he had been trading a long time with the Cheyenne, whom he loved, and who was brother to the Arapaho; that he only took what meat he wanted, and, pointing to his squaw, that his wife was Cheyenne. The Arapaho must not blame him. It was the whitemen from the States (Government men) with wagons, who scared the buffalo from him and his children. It was always his intention to live and die with the Cheyenne, for he had thrown away his brothers in the States. The Cheyenne lodge was his home—they smoked the same pipe—the broad prairie supported them both.

"The whiteman has forked tongue," replied the chief impatiently, raising his hand to his mouth, and sending it in a direct line with two of the fingers open and stretched far apart to signify a fork or divergence from a point.

I-sto-met, wah-hein ("p'shaw, no,") said Smith.

Ni-hi-ni, ni-hi-ni, Hook-ah-hay ("Yes, yes, good-bye,") and off they rode, trying, yet without much open manifestation, to drive our little band of horses with theirs, but by a dexterous interposition of Smith, he turned their heads, preventing the quiet trick of our brothers, the Arapahoes.

Smith told me after they left that they were just returning from a successful marauding expedition into New Mexico, with several scalps, two prisoners, and thirty or more horses and mules which they then had with them.[23]

Smith and Garrard had just arrived back at Bent's camp at the Big Timbers when word arrived of the Taos Rebellion during which Charles Bent, governor of New Mexico Territory, was murdered by Pueblo Indians. Garrard accompanied William Bent to the fort, there joining a group of mountain men who marched to Taos to revenge themselves against the Indians, thus parting company with John Smith for the rest of the winter.

It wasn't until the next spring, 1847, that Garrard, who had returned from New Mexico and joined an eastbound train at Bent's Fort, again met Smith, this time as the frontiersman came back into camp with a Cheyenne buffalo hunting party which he had led. To the young but now more experienced Garrard, Smith seemed even more "Indian" than ever, and it was with considerable surprise that he learned, when the train had straightened out, that Smith, his family, lodge dray, and horse herd were bringing up the rear of the caravan. The reason, he discovered, was that Smith had been engaged to take charge of Fort Mann, a new post being erected on the Santa Fe Trail twenty miles below the Cimarron Crossing as a way station for transportation and as protection to travelers against marauding Indians.

Though Smith was destined to continue a while longer as a Bent trader during the winter seasons and would remain closely associated with the Cheyennes, a new career lay ahead of him as official interpreter for both the Indian Bureau and the frontier army of the United States government.

---

[23] *Ibid.,* 164–66.

3

On the Santa Fe Trail

Once more the wagons were formed in the line of march, and the mules whipped into a brisk trot. Tom [John] Smith, with half a dozen mounted men, led the van; eighteen more rode abreast behind the wagons, to guard their rear; while the remaining horsemen galloped along side. Thus they moved on for a couple of miles, the Indians following close behind, but not yet venturing an attack. . .

Harper's New Monthly Magazine[1]

The Santa Fe Trail was first opened to trade in the fall of 1821 when William Becknell made the first journey with pack animals from Missouri to Santa Fe. He repeated the venture again the following year with twenty-one men and three wagons, and other traders began to follow. In May of 1824, the first wagon caravan bound for Santa Fe made up at Franklin, Missouri—83 men, 24 wagons and carts, and 200 horses. The train reached Santa Fe on July 28, its goods netting the traders some $180,000 in gold and silver, plus another $10,000 in furs. With successes of this sort, the trade began to flourish between the States and New Mexico, but the trail also served as one of the principal arteries of Western immigration as well as for government supply trains, exploring expeditions, and fur traders such as Bent and St. Vrain who yearly marketed their accumulation of furs, robes, mules, and horses

---

[1] "The Seige of Fort Atkinson," *Harper's New Monthly Magazine*, vol. 15 (October, 1857), 643.

in Missouri. As early as 1825, the government conducted an official survey of the Santa Fe Trail.

Landmarks and places of special interest soon began to develop names and identities, and trail incidents—some of which involved John Smith—sometimes made a particular locality famous to the men who were voyagers upon this inland journey through hostile territory. The diaries and logs of those who followed the rutted traces across Kansas and Colorado were usually written at night when camped at some landmark, recounting the sights, hardships, and adventures of the day.

Traveling the famous Santa Fe Trail during the mid-1800's, as did so many thousands of Americans headed to new lives in the West, was a monotonous, dreary, and wearisome experience spiced with moments of danger, adventure, and, sometimes, tragedy. Until the Civil War was ended in 1865 and the frontier military finally over-powered the wild tribes, the prairies of Kansas and Colo-rado were dominated by the Plains Indians: the Pawnees from the north, the Comanches and Kiowas to the south, the Cheyennes and Arapahoes who ranged on both sides of the Arkansas River, and other tribes whose war parties commonly visited the trail, sometimes to beg and some-times to plunder the transportation.

All in all, John Smith probably spent as much time on the road—with the Cheyennes, with Bent trains to and from Missouri, with the Indian agents who brought annu-ity goods to the tribes, and with the frontier military—as anyone. Though many of the adventures which Smith must have encountered on the trail have been lost to history, some of them have been recorded and passed on by those who knew the frontiersman.

Smith made many trips to Missouri with Bent caravans between 1838 and 1849. In the spring of each year, the

Bent traders would load the winter's haul of fur packs and
bales of buffalo robes onto the heavy wagons, hitch up a
six yoke of oxen to each, and head eastward up the long,
dry trail toward Westport. Accompanying the train also
would be a large herd of horses and mules to be sold at
Missouri settlements, while sometimes bands of Cheyennes and Arapahoes would ride with it as far as the
buffalo-hunting grounds at the Pawnee Fork.

The slow-moving trains, usually twenty to thirty wagons, generally traveled from early morning between break
of dawn and sunup until well past sundown. Only ten or
twelve miles a day were covered, depending upon the
availability of campsites with good grass, water, and
wood. Normally a halt for noon camp was made around
eleven o'clock and, if very hot, continued until two or
three o'clock in the afternoon to rest both the men and
animals. The wagons would be corralled and the stock
turned out to graze under the watchful eyes of herders,
just as was done each night.

The wagon train's company generally consisted of a
wagon master, who was in charge of the entire train; the
bullwhackers or teamsters, who drove the wagons; the
herders, who cared for both the oxen herd and the horse
and mule *caballada;* two or three hunters, who went out
on their own and were often waiting at the night's campsite with fresh buffalo or antelope meat; and the guards or
outriders whose jobs were principally to protect the train
against Indian attack. This was usually John Smith's job.

Upon leaving Bent's Fort, the caravan would follow
along the north bank of the Arkansas, never failing to
camp one night at the Big Timbers. Known to the Indians
as the "Pretty Encampment," the site possessed a grove of
tall, shady cottonwoods which lined the bank of the cool,
soft-flowing Arkansas. Here, on a rock bluff which jutted

into the river's course, William Bent constructed his new fort in 1853. In 1860 the government purchased the place and built Fort Wise, later to be renamed Fort Lyon. Few accounts of the trail by weary westbound travelers fail to mention this welcomed oasis at the Big Timbers.

From there the Bent trains would move past the mouth of Sand Creek, across the imaginary line established to separate Kansas and Colorado Territory in 1858, past Chouteau's Island where in 1816 Auguste Chouteau's party took refuge from a Pawnee war party, and to the Cimarron Crossing where the trail branched off southwestward to Santa Fe.

Beyond the crossing the military forts of Atkinson (1851), Dodge (1865), and Mann (1847) would see brief but exciting existences. Past Fort Mann, before the trail swung northeastward with the river, travelers would encounter the Caches, several large holes in the riverbank where in 1822 a party of traders had cached their goods while under an Indian attack.

Now the road crossed the mouth of Pawnee Fork, where Fort Larned would be constructed in 1859; then Ash Creek and on to the famous Pawnee Rock. Here a youthful Kit Carson shot his mule in mistake for an Indian in 1826. At Walnut Creek (later the site of Fort Zarah) the Santa Fe road left the Arkansas River and headed northeastward toward the Missouri River, passing as it went Cow Creek, the Little Arkansas, Dry Turkey Creek, Running Turkey Creek, Cottonwood Crossing, Lost Springs, Diamond Springs, and Council Grove, a heavily treed and serene location where wagon trains often banded together for protection and where an abundance of wood was available for wagon repairs. Now the train was in friendlier Kaw country the rest of the way, and the

men could stop watching each hill top for the sign of
mounted Indians and relax without fear of hearing a
spine-tingling war-whoop or the crack of a rifle.

Upon reaching Westport, after a journey of two or
three months, the bales of robes were unloaded on the
levee and the wagon train taken to a campsite outside of
town. Here the stock would be rested, and the men would
celebrate in the outlying saloons, such as the Last Chance
two miles south of Westport, with drinking, dancing,
gambling, and yarn-spilling.

William Bent, meanwhile, would take his furs by
steamboat down the Missouri River to St. Louis where he
would sell them to his lifelong friend, trader-merchant
Robert Campbell. Supplies for trail, trade, and fort would
be purchased and shipped back upstream to Westport
and loaded onto the wagons for the long return voyage
across the Kansas plains. The caravan would reach Bent's
Fort again in early autumn.[2]

In the year of 1844, a twenty-wagon Bent's Fort train
was accompanied by Cheyenne Chief Slim Face, who
wished to complain to the government about the selling
of liquor to his tribe by unscrupulous traders and about
the killing of buffalo calves by whites on the prairies. The
Bent party arrived in St. Louis on July 18, 1844, by
steamer with 700 packs of buffalo robes and four packs of
beaver furs.[3]

Lieutenant J. W. Abert, who was a visitor to Bent's Fort
two summers later, got the story of Slim Face's stay in St.
Louis from John Smith:

> He [Slim Face] seems to have been best pleased with the
> riding and the horses that he saw one evening at a circus. He

---

[2] Grinnell, *Bent's Old Fort*, 25–28.
[3] Washington *Daily National Intelligencer*, July 8, 1844.

recollects perfectly every horse that appeared, and gives an account of the colors, marks, and trappings of each one of them, with extra ordinary exactness and minuteness of detail. To see the whites ride so well, was to him almost incomprehensible, and was the only superiority that he would admit that the civilized man had derived from his civilization, when compared to his own rude manners of life. He wondered much, too, to see so many people living in one town, so far from any hunting grounds. Wishing one day to ascertain exactly the number of inhabitants, he procured a long square stick, and set himself down on the pavement to note the passers by cutting a notch in his stick for each one; and he commenced counting, and counted, and counted, but as the busy stream of the multitudes flowed on undiminished, the Indian was obliged to give up his inclination and now threw away the stick that he had at first resolved to take home and show his people.[4]

Until Fort Mann was constructed in 1847, the Santa Fe Trail was void of any military posts, way stations, or settlements of any kind all the way from Westport to Bent's Fort. This meant that the road traversed over 600 miles of prairie which was dominated by wild tribes, without a single place to seek refuge or replenish exhausted supplies. Transportation along the route was harassed constantly by marauding bands of hostiles, as if the trip were not difficult enough already with swollen streams, seas of prairie mud, droughts, sickness, trail accidents, lawless renegades, and other hazards of frontier travel.

Even without the Indians it was a long and difficult journey, and it was because of this that the War Department contracted a wagon master named Mann to construct a post on the trail just down from the Cimarron Crossing. Still, it was easier to build the fort than to find men to garrison it. When the position of commander of the post was offered to John Smith in the spring of 1847,

---

[4] W. H. Emory, *Notes of a Military Reconnaissance*, 423–24.

the Indian trade was through for the summer, and with no other employment at hand he reluctantly accepted.[5]

Workmen were still busy making bricks for chimney construction when Smith and Garrard arrived with the eastbound train on May 15, 1847. The fort consisted of four long houses which were connected by timber stockade walls about twenty feet in height, with loopholes cut in them for small arms and the one six-pounder which the garrison owned. Two large gates, each a foot thick, swung on wooden hinges. In diameter Fort Mann was about sixty feet, encompassing, among other things, a blacksmith shop for the repair of wagons.

One of the men at the fort had only recently been shot and lanced by Comanches as he was fishing in the river which was not three hundred feet away and in plain view of forty armed men. The Indians had ridden away hooting and screeching with the man's scalp waving in the air. And only two days before, the Indians had stolen fifteen yoke of oxen and forty mules picketed close to the fort, losing a brave in the effort.

For the teamsters working there, these attacks added emphasis to the fact that Fort Mann was a long, long way from civilization and that the Indians could have them any time they decided to try. It was only with a great deal of persuasion that eight of them finally agreed to remain and guard the fort, at thirty dollars a month and rations. These eight, plus Garrard, who decided he had never seen an Indian fight and this was a good chance, remained behind when the wagon train left, comprising the garrison command of "Captain" John Simpson Smith, Commander of Fort Mann.

Thus, with nine men, one cannon, forty rounds of grape

[5] Garrard, Wah-to-Yah, 327.

and canister, forty cannon cartridges, six rifles, and seven
muskets, Smith and his crew were, as Garrard put it,
". . . a small band to guard a fort in the Pawnee and
Comanche range—both tribes noted for their dexterity
and willingness to take the whiteman's 'hair' or his caballada."[6]

Smith proceeded to establish a watch schedule for the
fort, assigning the first guard to himself and Garrard. One
can easily imagine the trepidation felt by the two men as
they walked their posts that night, surrounded as they
were by a lonely and hostile land. Garrard describes it
well:

> Standing guard was anything but pleasant, and at night ex-
> ceedingly dreary. Smith would mount post on the roof for a
> while, and I down below would creep from port to port, now
> listening for the foe—now seated on the cannon, holding my
> breath at the least sigh of the winds. In pacing my lonely walk, I
> was filled with gloomy forebodings. The wind whistled a mourn-
> ful tune—the damp, fitful gusts nearly overturned me in their
> suddenness. Scarce fifteen yards distant, brutal wolves fought
> over the grave of the murdered man.[7]

Later, when a guard fell asleep on his post, Smith gave
him a reprimand and threatened the next time to tie the
man across the cannon and give a severe jerking.

But Smith's heart was not with it. To remain long in
such confinement and strict routine was too much against
his nature. He had lived on the wild frontier too long to
tolerate a situation where it was so easy to lose both his
stock and his hair. Thus when a Bent and St. Vrain wagon
train arrived at Fort Mann on the twenty-third of May,
Smith turned the command over to another and headed
east with the train. He took with him two mules belonging to Garrard, with the intention of letting them graze

---

[6] *Ibid.*, 335.   [7] *Ibid.*, 336.

along the way, then returning them to Fort Mann with a westbound train.

Thus, in little over a week's time, Smith had ended his career as a fort commander, though his adventures for this trip were by no means ended.

Traveling with the Bent train was trader William Tharpe, who during the past winter had also conducted trading activities at the Big Timbers. When the train reached Walnut Creek, an attack by Comanches resulted in the deaths of Tharpe and another frontiersman named McGuire, as well as the loss of Smith's seven mules and the two belonging to Garrard.

Garrard's account of this, obviously dependent on hearsay, states merely that Tharpe had gone buffalo hunting about two hundred yards from the train when he was jumped by four parties of Indians. Tharpe held them off for a time but was eventually killed and scalped.

The full details of the fight are not known, but Tharpe's death is evidently the basis for a story which John Smith told around the campfires of his later years. A reporter for the *Chicago Tribune* who met Smith at the Medicine Lodge peace council in 1867 tells the story this way:

> Lo Smith, the Cheyenne interpreter, who has been thirty years in this country, would on no account, shoot a quail, since, on one occasion when he went out to shoot buffalo, and had his gun lifted, a quail lit on the barrel. He was frightened and went to the fort. Soon after two men went out after buffalo and were shot by Indians who were hiding in the bank.[8]

That this was the Tharpe incident finds support in a story told by Colonel Henry Inman, who knew Smith during the Sheridan-Custer campaign in Indian Territory in

---

[8] *Chicago Tribune*, October 24, 1867. *The Missouri Republican*, June 17, 1847, reported that Frank De Lisle was also killed and that Smith lost seven animals during the attack at Walnut Creek. The train was listed as belonging to Bent, St. Vrain & Co.

1868–69. Despite the fact that Inman obviously embellishes the account considerably, he places the time as June, 1847, and the place as Pawnee Bottom near Pawnee Rock, both of which are correct for Garrard's incident, though he does mistake the dead man's name as "Thorp."[9]

Inman repeats the Smith "quail" yarn as supposedly the frontiersman told it to him, but makes several errors regarding Smith's activities prior to the incident, stating that he had just come down from the Yellowstone country where he had been trapping for two seasons. This is not so, of course.

George Bent claims that during this summer of 1847 his father's train was encamped on Pawnee Fork and was attacked by a war party of Comanches under Red Arm or Red Sleeve. This chief was killed, with both John Smith and Thomas Murphy claiming it was his shot which knocked the Comanche off his horse.[10]

Whether Smith made it on in to Westport or whether he tagged onto a westbound caravan following the murder of Tharpe is not clear. By September of 1847 he was in Santa Fe, about to begin a new career as a guide and interpreter for the first Cheyenne and Arapaho Indian agency. One way or another, he evidently did not meet Garrard again. The young adventurer remained at Fort Mann himself only until about the middle of June, at which time he joined a States-bound caravan which carried a friend of his father.

Another Inman tale concerning John Smith on the Santa Fe Trail is dated somewhat vaguely as "June, 1845,

---

[9] Colonel Henry Inman, *The Old Santa Fe Trail* (New York: The Macmillan Company, 1897), 300–304. Garrard makes several mentions of Tharpe, his Mexican wife, and two children whom he met at the Big Timbers.

[10] George E. Hyde, *Life of George Bent Written From His Letters*, Savoie Lottinville, ed., (Norman, Oklahoma: University of Oklahoma Press, 1967), 265–66.

if I don't disremember."[11] Supposedly, Smith and three other men were headed for Missouri and had camped near the present site of Fort Dodge, where the trappers were witnesses to an attack by Pawnee Indians upon a Mexican bull train en route from Santa Fe to the States.

As they watched, a man, woman, and small boy jumped out of one wagon and ran to escape, but the Indians killed the husband and scalped him and took the woman prisoner. As one Indian reached to capture the boy, one of the trappers pulled up his rifle and knocked the buck from his horse.

The trappers saved the boy, who said his name was Paul Dale and that his father had been a missionary among the Mexicans at Santa Fe. Smith and the others took the boy on with them to Independence, where they sold their goods and waited more than two months for a St. Vrain train to return to New Mexico. During this time Smith became very attached to the boy, who stayed with Smith's aunt during the time. The frontiersman bought Paul Dale a coal-black pony and then dressed him up with a suit of buckskin and white sombrero.

In August Smith and the boy returned to Bent's Fort on the Arkansas, camping on arrival just outside the fort. When they went inside to purchase some goat's milk, a white woman ran up and threw her arms around Paul. It was the boy's mother who Smith later learned had escaped her Pawnee captors and on a stolen horse had made it back to the Santa Fe Trail where she was picked up by an American group headed for Taos. Smith supposedly gave the boy two hundred dollars as he departed with his mother for Pennsylvania and never saw the lad again.

The yarn certainly smacks strongly of "frontier fancy,"

---

[11] Inman, 283–99.

whether Smith's or Inman's, and has no corroboration from other sources.

Inman also tells a tale involving Smith on Frenchman's Creek in the summer of 1846 wherein Smith helped save some friends who were captured by the Sioux. In typical frontier tall-tale style, the account quotes Smith as stating: "Ike, who was a right fine shot and had killed three at one time, said: 'I always like to get two or three of the red devils in a line before I pull the trigger; it saves lead.' "[12]

A story concerning Smith that might be accepted with more credence, despite some error in name, appeared in an 1857 issue of *Harper's New Monthly Magazine*.[13] Written by a Charles Hallock, who accompanied a Bent train returning from Independence to Fort St. Vrain on the South Platte by way of the Arkansas route, "The Siege of Fort Atkinson" suffers from some obvious misnaming of people—"Charles" rather than "Tom" Fitzpatrick, "Tom" rather than "John" Smith—but otherwise it appears to be a valid description of the people, places, and events.

With Fort Mann having "gone under" in 1847, the government had since constructed Fort Atkinson in 1850—built of adobe bricks and roofed with canvas—and in the summer of 1852 it was garrisoned with ninety Sixth Regiment infantry and twenty First Dragoons. As had been designated by Fitzpatrick, then agent for the Cheyennes and Arapahoes, Atkinson was to be the distribution point for annuity goods to the Kiowas and Comanches. Some 10,000 Indians were camped along the river, including some Cheyennes and Arapahoes, impatiently waiting for Fitzpatrick and the goods and becoming increasingly hostile as the hot days passed.

[12] *Ibid.*, 305–13.   [13] "The Seige of Fort Atkinson," 638–48.

The small garrison received the brunt of the Comanche-Kiowa anger, and it was only through the efforts of a chief, whose name was given as Yellow Bear, that a massacre of the fort was prevented. It was into this boiling situation that a Bent train, with John Smith along, arrived from the States in July.

Bent's train consisted of fourteen white-tilted Conestoga wagons, drawn mostly by mules though five were pulled by oxen, six to a wagon. Accompanying the wagons were two light carriages, rare upon the prairie, carrying a group of young adventurers out to see the West, plus a number of mounted frontiersmen who carefully guarded the pack animals and seventy head of loose stock. All in all, there were only about fifty persons in the train, but it was well organized and amply protected against Indian attack.

Indian signs had been scarce, but as the train neared Fort Atkinson Indians from the Comanche and Kiowa camps began swarming about the train, though not molesting it. Since his family was with him, Bent hurried forward with his five wagons and the carriages with enough men to protect them, leaving behind the remaining wagons under guard of sixteen men.

Almost as soon as Bent was gone, the Indians began trying to stampede the wagon train and horse herd, galloping close while they whooped and yelled, rattled their spears against the tough buffalo hide of their shields, and shook their robes in the faces of the train stock. But the train guards, John Smith among them, were old, experienced teamsters and hunters who refused to be panicked by the Indians. They rode steadily alongside the train in lines, their rifle bores promising sure death to the first brave who went too far.

Within eight miles of the fort, however, it became apparent that it would be necessary to send to the fort for help:

> There remained no alternative but to send to the fort for help, dangerous as the expedient was, and offering but a bare possibility of success; for the courier had a fearful gauntlet to run through such a multitude of savages, who, at once divining his intent, would attempt to cut him off. Nevertheless, a volunteer was immediately found in Tom [John] Smith, a veteran trapper, who rode a noble mustang of the finest mettle.
>
> "I'll risk it," he said. "Thar's good grit in old 'Lightfoot' yet, and she's seen red skin afore; eh, old gal?" and bending forward, he patted his favorite steed upon the neck, which salutation she returned with a low whinney of pleasure. Then drawing up the reins, he trotted her easily a few rods, then striking his spurs into her flanks, dashed on toward the fort with lightning speed. She was a noble beast. Many a time she had saved him from the vengeance of the savages, and now she bore him safely to the fort, distancing the few who attempted to pursue. Bent's wagons had but just arrived as Tom [John] came up, having experienced but little trouble from the Indians, owing no doubt, to the presence of Yellow Bear, who proved an excellent passport to the whites who he befriended.[14]

Bent and Smith, accompanied by the twenty dragoons, rode immediately to the beleaguered train which had now been formed into a horseshoe shape with the caballada inside for protection. The Comanches and Kiowas fell back before Bent's angry threats.

In this fashion the train finally made it safely to Fort Atkinson, where Bent soothed the angry Indians by opening a barrel of sugar and feeding it out to the chiefs and headmen of the bands. About that time word arrived that troops were approaching the fort. The Indian camps immediately began to disband, and by morning the last teepee had disappeared from view along the Arkansas. On

---

[14] *Ibid.*, 642.

the following day two companies of mounted riflemen arrived at Fort Atkinson.

Such incidents, though often exaggerated by those who told them secondhand, were undoubtedly commonplace in the life of John Smith. It was much to Smith's distinction merely that he managed to survive for forty years in a savage world where life or death often hung on the slender thread of a look, a word, or a move.

Traveling with the same wagon train as had John Smith and Garrard in the spring of 1847 was Englishman George Frederick Ruxton, who later wrote a book entitled *Life in the Far West*. Ruxton strangely makes no mention of Smith, mentioning almost every other important name of that time and place. It is, of course, possible that Ruxton had only a passing awareness of the frontiersman and chose to ignore him. Or it may be possible, as historian LeRoy R. Hafen discusses in an appendix to *Life in the Far West*, that Smith was the prototype for Ruxton's fictitious character, "Killbuck," who plays so prominent a role in the book.[15]

Most of the other frontiersmen of the day, Hafen argues, were mentioned in the book by their own names: Joe Walker, Bill Williams, William Bent, Dick Wootton, Black Harris, John Hatcher, Rube Herring, and Jim Waters. Others, such as Thomas Fitzpatrick, Kit Carson, James Bridger, Philip Thomas, and Joe Meek, were known to be elsewhere at the time.

Hafen lists certain parallels between Smith and the Killbuck which Ruxton describes: both were native Kentuckians, both were well-seasoned trappers and traders, their first squaws were Blackfeet, the traits of hardness and cruelty combined with kindness and decency in both men, both were yarn-spillers of the first class, and both,

---

[15] Ruxton, 240–44.

supposedly, were present on the Arkansas at the time Ruxton passed by.

There are, however, a number of discrepancies between the real John Smith and the fictional Killbuck. John Smith was married and with his family at the time; Killbuck had no family with him. Killbuck was partner with La Bonte; Smith was very much a lone wolf. Killbuck was described as having taken part in many adventures which Smith is not known to have ever mentioned. Killbuck had wounds which Smith is not known to have suffered.

Ruxton stated that the characters in his book are "real (the names being changed in two or three instances only, and all have been, and are well known in the Western country.)" But he also admitted that ". . . I have, no doubt, jumbled the dramatic personae, one with another . . ."[16]

Whether or not Killbuck is really a dramatization of John Smith, all or in part, will never be answered with certainty. It is doubtful that Ruxton, who spent the winter of 1846 and the spring of 1847 at Fort Pueblo just upriver from Bent's place, could have failed to meet or hear mention of John Smith or would have chosen to completely ignore him. But from the descriptions of Smith by Garrard and by other writers and by virtue of his background as a free trader and experience with the Indians, there can be little doubt that he was an excellent prototype of the frontiersman of the mid-1800's.

---

[16] *Ibid.*, xvi.

4

Talking for the White Father

Before leaving Santa Fe, I met with the man who I had all along intended to engage as interpreter for the Chyennes and Aripohoes, he having been in charge at Fort Mann at the time of its abandonment, and the garrison being reduced to seven men, he was obliged, like myself to keep with the current of travel, and got to Santa Fe a short time before us. I engaged him for three months, only at twenty-five dollars per month, for the purpose of making an excursion with me amongst the Chyenne and Aripohoes. . .   Agent Thomas Fitzpatrick[1]

The problem of controlling the wild tribes on the Central Plains in the face of ever-increasing immigration and transportation along the Arkansas and Platte trails was recognized by the government as a serious one. Someone was needed who could hold the tribes in restraint, who knew the country and the Indians well, and who could prevent trouble before it arose. The man chosen for this momentous task was mountain man Thomas Fitzpatrick, "Broken Hand" as the Indians knew him, who was named in 1846 as the first agent for the newly created Upper Platte and Arkansas Rivers Agency. As such he became responsible for the welfare of thousands of Americans who would cross the prairies during the coming years, including the great flood of gold-seekers who rushed headlong for California in 1849.

---

[1] "Appendix to the Report of the Commissioner of Indian Affairs," 30 Cong., 1st sess., *Senate Executive Document I*, Fitzpatrick to Harvey, Sept. 18, 1847, 241.

Fitzpatrick knew the frontier as well as any man, and he knew his Indians, too. But Fitzpatrick was badly in need of someone who was particularly acquainted with the Sioux, Cheyennes, and Arapahoes, spoke their languages, and was trusted by them. John Simpson Smith fit that bill perfectly.

It was by curious luck that the two men happened to meet in Santa Fe during the summer of 1847, having barely missed one another on the trail. After leaving Fort Mann, joining an eastbound train and being involved in the Tharpe affair, Smith attached himself and his family to the first westbound train he met, one which took the Cimarron Cutoff to Santa Fe. At almost the same time, but with a different train, Fitzpatrick arrived on the Arkansas for the purpose of visiting the tribes and arranging for a peace treaty with them. Traveling with an escort of dragoons bound for Santa Fe, the newly appointed agent reached Fort Mann in July, finding it a total wreck and abandoned. Because of this he had to give up his plan of remaining there until he could find escort to Bent's Fort and instead continued on with the dragoons via the Cimarron route to Santa Fe, thus, like Smith, ending up where he had no previous intention of being. But there he came across John Smith, whom he hired as a guide and interpreter among the Cheyennes and Arapahoes for the summer.

> This is the only way that men of that description can be engaged for the sum that the department allows for that purpose; and it is only when they are disengaged that they can be had on such terms—the traders pay them more for the winter's trade, besides finding them in provisions, &c., than the department allows for the whole year. However, under the present circumstances, and while so many different tribes are to be dealt with, all speaking different tongues, the mode I have adopted, and intend for the future to adopt, is the best and most economi-

cal. Good interpreters value their services in this country at a high rate; but no man of any kind, could be hired here at three hundred dollars per annum, without provisioning him also.[2]

John Smith accepted the position and accompanied Fitzpatrick to Bent's Fort, beginning a new career as a government interpreter which he was to follow, off and on, for the rest of his life.

Upon their arrival at the fort, the head men of the Cheyennes and Arapahoes were called into a council. After a small feast of bread, coffee, and other items donated by Bent, Fitzpatrick made a speech to the Indians, with Smith interpreting, advising them to stop their plundering and warring with other tribes and to turn to agriculture to provide their subsistence.[3]

Chief Yellow Wolf answered through Smith that the Cheyennes were willing to try to raise corn, but that they would need help since they did not know how. He requested that the great father in Washington be told the Cheyennes were willing to obey his word and to fight with the whites against the Comanches. He asked, too, that the great father be told about the killing of Cinemo, or "Old Tobacco," a chief who had always been a good friend to the whites and with whom Smith and Garrard had stayed during that winter of 1846–47.

The killing of Cinemo was a prime example of why an agent such as Fitzpatrick was needed on the frontier and just how valuable a man of Smith's experience could be in understanding and interpreting the talk and the true feelings of the Indians.[4]

During the spring of 1846, a government train was passing along the Arkansas River, unaware that a hostile band of Comanches was in the neighborhood with the intention of plundering the train. Cinemo heard about it

[2] *Ibid.*   [3] *Ibid.*, 242.   [4] *Ibid.*, 242–43.

and rode to the wagon train to warn it. A guard on the caravan saw him coming and waved at him to "go back." But in Cheyenne, to raise the hands above the head and bring them down in a fashion similar to the way the guard made his motion was a sign to "come quickly" to the Indians. The old chief complied and kicked his pony in a gallop toward the train. The guard, completely green in the ways of the West, panicked and opened fire, mortally wounding Cinemo.

Before dying five days later, the Cheyenne chief called his family together and told them that he knew it was all a mistake and not to seek revenge. Still, when Fitzpatrick and Smith arrived, Chief Yellow Wolf expressed concern that the white man had not, as Indian custom demanded, "dryed up the tears" over Cinemo's death with a restitution payment. Failure to do so often resulted in war among the families or tribes involved in such incidents.

Fitzpatrick, undoubtedly taking Smith's recommendation on the matter, accepted the Cheyennes as being sincere in their expressions of friendship for the whites, though he was skeptical of their ability to change from their life-by-the-hunt to an agricultural existence. He was much concerned over the debauchery of the Indians by those nefarious traders who plied the Indians with whiskey. In fact, when he and Smith left Bent's Fort the following season, 1848, on the South Platte, Fitzpatrick seized two kegs of whiskey from a white trader there and dumped them into the river.[5]

The agent returned to the Arkansas again in the spring of 1849, where Smith again assisted him in talking with the tribal chiefs, this time at the Big Timbers. In August

---

[5] LeRoy R. Hafen, "Thomas Fitzpatrick and the First Indian Agency in Colorado," *The Colorado Magazine*, vol. VI, no. 2, 35–62. Citing Report of June 24, 1848, Upper Platte File; H 545, Indian Dept. Archives.

Fitzpatrick was ordered to Washington, D.C., by Superintendent of Indian Affairs D. D. Mitchell to help urge the
Congress to hold a peace council with the principal tribes
of the Plains and Rocky Mountains. Congress did allocate
funds for this purpose, and on June 1, 1851, Fitzpatrick
and Smith arrived at Ft. Atkinson on the Missouri,[6] a post
established by Colonel E. V. Sumner near present Dodge
City, Kansas, in August of 1850.

They found the river dried up and the few pools of
stagnant water so polluted with dead fish that even the
thirsty stock would not drink from them. Fitzpatrick immediately dispatched runners in all directions, and within
two weeks the entire countryside on both banks of the
river was filled with lodges belonging to the Kiowas, Comanches, Plains Apaches, Arapahoes, and Cheyennes.

Fitzpatrick and Smith held separate feasts with each
tribe, the fare consisting of bread, pork, and coffee, and
distributed small presents to the chiefs of each. Fitzpatrick then gave a talk, inviting each to attend a grand
council of the Plains tribes at Fort Laramie on the first
day of September.

Despite promises that a large quantity of goods would
be distributed at the council, the Kiowas, Comanches,
and Plains Apaches refused to risk taking their horse
herds so far into the country of such famous horse-stealers
as the Crows and Sioux. The Cheyennes and Arapahoes,
however, agreed to attend and immediately began making
preparations for the trip northward.

It was at this point in the council that the services of
John Smith took on even greater value. One of the officers
attached to the command of Colonel Sumner took it on
himself to severely flog a Cheyenne brave who he felt had

---

[6] *Report of Commissioner of Indian Affairs, 1851*, 334–35. Thomas Fitzpatrick,
Washington City, November 24, 1851.

been guilty of unseemly conduct toward the officer's wife. Actually the brave was Lean Bear, later to become a principal chief of the Cheyenne nation, who had become overly fascinated by a ring on the woman's hand.

The Cheyennes, who did not believe in striking their male children for fear of breaking the warrior spirit, were greatly incensed by the officer's action, taking it as an insult to the entire tribe. The Comanches and Kiowas, always interested in a good fight, claimed the Cheyennes were planning an attack in retaliation, and Fitzpatrick requested that Sumner station his troops near the Cheyenne camp in a show of strength.

The Cheyennes, now alarmed at the turn of events, came to the agent and, talking through John Smith, denied that they had any intention of attacking. The matter was diplomatically settled by presenting Lean Bear with a blanket to soothe his wounds.[7]

Fitzpatrick and Smith left the Arkansas on July 3 and arrived at Fort Laramie on the twenty-fifth. At the same time, the Indians began to gather: Cheyennes, Arapahoes, Ogallalah and Brule Sioux, Shoshonis, Snakes, Assiniboines, Minnitarees, Arikaras, and Crows. Before the treaty council had been completed, over ten thousand Indians had gathered at this first great assembly of the Plains Indian tribes.[8]

---

[7] Hyde, *Life of George Bent*, 98. See also George Bent Letters, Yale University, Berthrong Collection, Oklahoma University Division of Manuscripts. Letter dated Feb. 19, 1913. Donald J. Berthrong, *The Southern Cheyennes* (Norman: University of Oklahoma Press, 1963), 117.

[8] St. Louis *Daily Missouri Republican*, Oct. 24, 1851. This account of the Ft. Laramie Treaty utilizes accounts which appeared in the St. Louis *Daily Missouri Republican*, September 26 through November 10, 1851; LeRoy R. Hafen and Francis Marion Young, *Fort Laramie and the Pageant of the West*, 1834–1890 (Glendale, Calif: The Arthur H. Clark Co., 1938); Percival G. Lowe, *Five Years a Dragoon, '49 to '54 and Other Adventures on the Great Plains* (Kansas City: Franklin Hundson Printing Co., 1906).

Superintendent of Indian Affairs Mitchell, escorted by a company of dragoons, arrived on August 30. Bringing his Shoshonis from the Green River country was the famous Jim Bridger, while the renowned missionary and Western explorer, Father de Smet, arrived in the company of the Crows. The editor of the *Missouri Republican*, A. B. Chambers, and a reporter named B. Gratz Brown, later to serve as a congressman from Missouri and run as vice-presidential candidate on Greeley's Liberal Republican ticket, were on hand, writing extensive reports of the treaty spectacular.

John Smith was the official interpreter for the Cheyennes at the Fort Laramie treaty council and, as such, was an official signer of the treaty document. He obviously played a key role in the activities of council, translating the talk of Fitzpatrick and the commissioners into guttural Cheyenne sounds and sign language, interpreting the speeches of the Cheyenne chiefs into English, carefully explaining away misunderstandings. A typical incident took place when the Snakes, bitter enemies of the Cheyennes, arrived. Catching a Snake man and his boy away from their camp, a Cheyenne party killed and scalped them. The Snakes put up their death howl, and to settle this crisis a special meeting had to be called. Chambers and Brown described the affair.

> Soon after the breaking up of the Council, the Snakes marched up to the Cheyenne village, distant about a mile. Upon arriving there, they were seated in an arbor, formed of a number of lodge skins and poles, forming a semi-circle, about one-half open to the east. Around the sides, skins and mats had been placed for the Snakes and the whites to sit upon. The guests occupied about half the circle; the remainder was occupied by the Cheyennes. On one side were the Cheyenne chiefs, as fine specimens of men as can be found anywhere; on the other sat a large company of soldiers, (young men) several rows deep.

These men seem to be physically better developed, and have more expression and manifest more intelligence, than most of the other Indians.

A considerable time elapsed before the ceremonies commenced. This interval was occupied in smoking, but no conversation took place between the Indians. At length, the *Porcupine Bear* came in, and made a speech to his people, principally to his young men, urging them to treat the Snakes as friends—to smoke with them, take them by the hand, and give them presents. He was peculiarly forcible, judging from his gestures and the translation of his speech by the interpreter Smith. He urged the young men to listen to the counsel and advice of the old men and, in the future, never to go to war, or do any other act without the permission of the chiefs. After a while, the old men outside commenced to harangue the village, and soon they began to collect from all quarters.[9]

Boiled mashed corn in a large copper kettle was brought in and passed out to the Snakes, and after much speech-making, presenting of gifts, and ceremony during which the scalps of the Snakes were returned, the meeting evolved into an orgy of brotherly dancing and singing which lasted far into the night.

Because of the enormous number of Indians, all of them with large horse herds which needed forage, the council site was moved to Horse Creek several miles below Fort Laramie. When all of the tribes had finally been assembled, preparations were made for the first council on the morning of September 10. Everyone, Indians and whites alike, was anxious for the event, and even at dawn the prairie was alive with moving masses of chiefs, warriors, women, and children, some on horseback, some on foot. At nine o'clock the dragoon escort fired its cannon, and Old Glory was hoisted above the camp.

From the Indian camps came the principal men of the tribes, followed by younger men on horseback. Behind

[9] St. Louis *Daily Missouri Republican*, Oct. 29, 1851.

them came the squaws and children, each nation dressed in full regalia, making its own peculiar demonstration and singing tribal songs. Their horses and equipment were ornamented with fancy trappings, while the warriors themselves, though not painted for war, were decked out in their finest, each competing in his efforts to be elegant, fashionable, and exquisite. The squaws, too, were dressed in their finest costumes: all varieties of wild animal furs, beads, porcupine quills, and multicolored cloths.

The council ground was a huge circle with an arbor constructed in the center with an opening to the east. Only the principal men were allowed to take a seat inside, while the braves took positions behind their chiefs and behind them the rest of the tribe. The tribes were arranged in the order of the Sioux, the Cheyennes, the Assiniboines, the Shoshonis, the Arikaras, the Gros Ventres, the Mandans, and then the Arapahoes.

The Crows arrived late, mounted on jaded but beautiful animals, singing their songs, with two principal chiefs riding in front carrying highly ornamented pipes and followed by their warriors—all well armed—and a few women. The Crows were assigned a place in the council and seated themselves calmly amid their most hated enemies.

In the middle were seated Colonel Mitchell, Major Fitzpatrick, the commissioners, the military officers, Father de Smet, the interpreters such as John Smith and Jim Bridger, and others. Once the Indians had taken their places, following the custom which they all followed in their own councils, they ceased their chanting and singing and the council became as quiet as if in church.

> Tobacco was handed round to all the chiefs and braves in council, and then we had a general smoke. This custom seems to be observed in the same manner by all. The principal chief rolls his redstone pipe full of tobacco and kinnekinick, and after

lifting it east, west, north and south, and up to the Great Spirit, takes a smoke himself, and it is passed around for all others to smoke. All of one tribe or band, and their friends who are present, smoked from the same pipe.[10]

Speeches were made by the chiefs of the various tribes, all professing their friendship and desire for peace, telling of how destitute were their people, and saying they hoped the treaty goods, which had been delayed by heavy rains on the trail, would soon arrive. As had been previously requested by the commission, each tribe announced their selection of a principal chief, and the Cheyennes named theirs as *Wan-ne-sah-tah*, or "Who walks with his toes turned out," the great medicine man of the tribe. A council was held on the following day with the Crows alone.

Though reporter Brown was favorably impressed by the Cheyennes, he could not quite stomach one of their customs:

> This evening, in the Cheyenne's camp, for the first time, I witnessed the interesting process of killing and dressing a dog for a feast. The victim was a large cur, quite fat. Two squaws lassoed him and struck him until he was dead. They then put him on a fire, and singed, or rather roasted off the hair, scraping the skin until it was as clean as a scalded hog. They then dressed it, and cut it up, and put it into a large copper kettle, where it was boiled until the bones came out. Having witnessed the process of preparation, I could not indulge in the luxury of eating any of it.[11]

Undoubtedly, John Smith, who had once fooled Garrard into eating dog by telling him it was turtle, was highly amused at the whites who became quite ill from the Cheyenne delicacy.

Colonel Mitchell requested the interpreters, traders, and trappers who were familiar with the Indian country to meet with him and the principal men of each tribe to

---

[10] *Daily Missouri Republican*, Sept. 26, 1851.   [11] *Ibid.*, Oct. 5, 1851.

determine the boundaries of the territories of the respective nations. Father de Smet, James Bridger, and John Smith were among those present whose vast experience and travel in the Western wilderness contributed much to the final designations of tribal territories. At a council on the thirteenth, Black Hawk, an Ogallalah Sioux, made a speech objecting to the North Platte as a boundary line between the Sioux and the Cheyenne and Arapaho range and to the Cheyenne desire to hunt north of the Platte. He claimed that the Sioux had whipped both the Crows and the Kiowas and run them out of that country, that the Ogallalah had helped the Cheyennes and Arapahoes defeat the Kiowas at Crow Creek, and that they deserved the right to hunt south of the river. Mitchell finally convinced him that fixed boundary lines would not restrict hunting parties so long as they remained peaceful.

The final result was that the Cheyennes and Arapahoes were given all the land between the North Fork of the Platte and the Arkansas River, from the mountains into western Kansas. The Cheyennes' attitude was expressed by the Bear's Feather in a speech translated to the commissioner by Smith:

I am glad to see so many Indians and whites meeting in peace. It makes my heart glad, and I shall be more happy at home. I am glad you have taken pity on us, and come to see us. The buffalo used to be plenty in our country, but it is getting scarce. We got enough to come here and to keep us a while, but our meat will not last long. As the sun looks down upon us—(so) the Great Spirit sees me I am willing, Grand Father, to do as you tell me to do. I know you will tell me right, and that it will be good for me and my people. We regard this as a great *medicine day*, when our pipes and water shall be one, and we all shall be at peace. Our young men, Grand Father, whom you want to go with you to the States, are ready, and they shall go. I shall look to their return when the grass begins to grow again. If all the nations here were as willing to do what you tell them, and do what they say as we are, then we could sleep in peace; we would not have to watch our horses or our lodges in the night.[12]

On the seventeenth of September, 1851, the treaty was drawn up and ready for the signatures of the Indian chiefs and government commissioners. Smith instructed the Cheyennes where to make their marks and then added his own to the treaty paper as the interpreter, the first of four major treaties with these tribes which he was destined to sign. Three days after the signing, the treaty goods arrived and were distributed. The chiefs now strutted around the camp in generals' uniforms, gilted swords dangling at their sides and their long hair hanging in braids down over their epaulets.

It had been decided that a delegation of the various tribes would be taken on a tour of the Eastern United States to impress them with the numbers and might of the country. Thirteen chiefs and prominent warriors were selected by the treaty commissioners and by the tribes. Three of them were Cheyennes—White Antelope, Little Chief, and Alights-on-the-Clouds—and John Smith was assigned to go along to Washington, D.C., as interpreter for them.

With the group in tow, Superintendent Mitchell, Fitzpatrick, Father de Smet, John Smith, and others departed the treaty grounds on September 23, arriving at Fort Kearny on the Platte River road on the second of October. Here Mitchell held a council between his entourage and twenty Pawnee chiefs and braves. For the Indians it was a historic meeting in peace between life-long enemies. Not only were the Cheyennes and Arapahoes the mortal enemies of the Pawnees, but so were the Sioux. Nonetheless, the Pawnees were hospitable and the meeting went well. At a banquet where there was much singing, dancing, and

---

[12] *Ibid.*, Nov. 3, 1851.

speech-making, Big Fatty of the Pawnee Loups told his enemies:

"Yes, my heart abounds with delight, for it had never dreamed of meeting you face to face, and of touching your hand in friendship. You see me here poor—I have not a horse to mount. Well, I will gladly go on foot the remainder of my day, if the tomahawk is to be buried by all."[13]

John Smith probably listened to this with tongue in cheek, knowing how many times the promises of peace between these tribes had been made before. Several of the Indians smoked the peace pipe with Big Fatty and made speeches of friendship, but when it came to Alights-on-the Clouds, the Cheyenne refused to smoke, stating that so far as he knew Cheyenne warriors might even then be raiding a Pawnee village and he would not betray his host by pretending there was peace between them.

From Kearny the group was led along the Kansas River to St. Mary's Mission in what was to be Kansas Territory by 1854. Their purpose was to let the wild Plains Indians see how other tribes, who were more domesticated, were succeeding with agricultural pursuits. At the mission the warriors were feasted on potatoes, carrots, turnips, squashes, parsnips, melons, apples, and peaches which had been raised by the Potawatomies. Afterward they were taken to church services, an experience just as unique to Smith as to the wild Indians with him.

Three days took the group to Westport, where on the sixteenth of October they boarded a steamboat for St. Louis. Their arrival in the city from whence John Smith had run away twenty-one years before was duly noted by the *Missouri Republican* on October 22:

---

[13] Hiram Martin Chittenden and Alfred Talbot Richardson, *Life, Letters and Travels of Father Pierre-Jean De Smet, S.J., 1801–1873*, 4 vols. (New York: F.D. Harper, 1905), vol. II, 687.

"Yesterday the Clara arrived in port, having on board Colonel Mitchell and Major Fitzpatrick the commissioner, Colonel Chambers, B. G. Brown, Colonel R. Campbell, the Reverend Father De Smedt, and a delegation of Indians from the plains in the charge of Mssrs. J. S. Smith and Joseph Tesson Honore, interpreters."[14]

The "fire canoe" had been a terrific experience for the Indians, who were badly frightened at first by the hissing, pounding steam engine. But once they were herded on deck and the boat began moving, the chiefs lost their fears. They seated themselves in full attire on the promenade deck, sang Indian songs, and waved and shouted to the amazed settlements that came into view along the river.

But as the Indians were led farther and farther away from their homes, they became more and more beset by homesickness and despondency. One of them, a Crow, disappeared and was found in the river near a landing with a deep stab wound in the neck over the left shoulder. Reporters were told that the Indian had committed suicide. Smith, nor any of the others who were in charge, said much about the quarrelsome nature of the Plains Indians.

The delegation arrived in Washington in mid-November, 1851. Here the savages of the Plains were lodged in the Maher Hotel, a trying experience for both the chiefs and their interpreters. Every effort was made to impress them during their stay. They were driven about in carriages, taken to tour the military forts, Navy yards, and the arsenal, and met by high government officials.[15]

On December 4, the Indians and their escorts were

[14] *Daily Missouri Republican*, Oct. 22, 1851.

[15] Washington *Daily National Intelligencer*, Nov. 19, Dec. 1, 5, 12, 13, 1851; Jan. 7, 9, 10, 1852.

taken to the Central Market in Washington, D.C., where they were amazed at the large quantity of both domestic and wild fowl for sale. One chief replenished his head dress with wing feathers of a large turkey.

The delegation was also taken to the White House, where it met with President Fillmore in a parlor, and John Smith had the honor of interpreting for the chief executive, the first of three presidents he would so serve. Fillmore urged the Indians to turn to agriculture. The chiefs requested horses and money, but the president replied that Fitzpatrick had funds for that and distributed silver peace medals and flags to the delegation. Two days later they were taken to Brown's Hotel where they were introduced to the famous exiled Hungarian patriot, Louis Kossuth.

The Indians and Smith alike were extremely happy to return to the Plains in January of 1852.

5

Back to Fort Laramie

The enclosed copy of inquiries of John S. Smith, Interpreter to Agent Twiss, answered under oath, before Agent Vaughn, is an additional indication that the real interests of the Government, as well as those of the Indians, have suffered from a general neglect on the part of the Indian Bureau. . .

Brig. General William S. Harney[1]

Sometime in the early fifties, John Smith left the Arkansas and took his squaw, his caballa, and son Jack and moved back north, once again using Fort Laramie as his base of operations. The trade had fallen off considerably on the Arkansas since Bent had destroyed his old fort with gunpowder in 1849, and the Indians were ranging farther away from both the Platte and the Arkansas roads along which white immigration was growing heavier daily. At Laramie a trader by the name of Elbridge Gerry, grandson of the signer of the Declaration of Independence, had been trading with the Northern Cheyennes for some time, and John Smith could be a big help to him in extending his operations to the South Platte region.[2]

---

[1] Letters Received, Office of Indian Affairs, 1824–81, Central Superintendency, Letter, March 23, 1856, Bvt. Brigadier General W. S. Harney, Headquarters Sioux Expedition, Fort Pierre, South Dakota.

[2] John Smith was still working for Bent in the fall of 1849 when the old fort was destroyed. A trading license dated August 11, 1849, lists Bent's employees as "John Smith, P. Carbonir, Charles McCue, J. Denison, V. Vasher, R. Fisher, B. Ritier, I. Sanders," and a ninth man whose name is illegible. National Archives, Ledgers of Licensed Indian Traders.

Trade had been conducted at Fort Laramie since 1834 when William Sublette and Robert Campbell, on their way to rendezvous, had stopped long enough to begin construction of a log-stockade fort, called Fort William, at the mouth of Laramie River.[3] The location had long been noticed as a likely spot: by Robert Stuart on his return trip from Astoria during the winter of 1812–1813; by Jim Bridger and Jedediah Smith in 1823; by Tom Fitzpatrick while returning to the States with a load of furs in 1830; by Zenas Leonard who told of a trappers' conclave there in 1832; and by Charles Larpenteur who described a drunken spree by hunters and trappers in 1833.

Only a year after construction, the post was purchased by Bridger, Fitzpatrick, and Milton Sublette, and in 1836 it was sold by them to the monopolistic American Fur Company and operated by Pierre Chouteau, Jr. In 1841 a rival post, Fort Platte, was constructed nearby on the south bank of the North Platte by Lieutenant Lancaster Lupton, and this competition caused Chouteau to construct a new adobe fort to replace the rotting Fort William. Named Fort John after John Sarpy, the post became more popularly known as Fort Laramie. Fort Platte was abandoned in 1845.

In June, 1848, the U.S. Army purchased Fort Laramie from the American Fur Company for $4,000 and garrisoned it with two officers and fifty-eight mounted riflemen under Major W. F. Sanderson. This was part of a plan by the government to provide protection for western emigrants by establishing a series of military stations on the route to Oregon. Fort Kearny, on the south bank of the Platte near the head of Grand Island in Nebraska, was also established in 1848.

---

[3] Hafen and Young, *Fort Laramie*, 26–28.

The immigration along the Platte road had increased tremendously during the forties—gold-seekers rushing headlong for California, settlers headed for the promised country of Oregon, and Mormons seeking a new land in Utah. By the fall of 1850 approximately 10,000 wagons had carried some 45,000 men, women, and children past Laramie, and by 1852 the tide had reached 40,000 annually, a quarter of them Mormons. The trail itself was littered with the carcasses and bones of dead draft animals and livestock, abandoned personal property, and broken down wagons and was dotted with the graves of those killed by the rigors of the trail or by disease and lack of sufficient food and water.

Mail service had begun around 1850, linking Laramie with the East and with Salt Lake City to the west. A toll bridge had been constructed over the Laramie River in 1852, and a better one in 1853 when the old one washed out during the spring rise. Travelers could cross at the cost of two dollars or three dollars per team, use the ferry at two dollars per wagon, or ford the river at their own peril. Emigrants generally halted their weary caravans across the river and came over to the fort to restock supplies, to post letters or pick up mail that had been forwarded to them there, to make minor repairs in the post's blacksmith shop, or to inquire about the Indian situation and the trail ahead.

John Smith must have watched this exodus of ox and mule-drawn wagons moving in never-ending succession along the river, with their white tops visible for miles, carrying weary but hopeful souls westward, and wondered, just as did the Indians, what it would all mean to the great life of freedom which the western mountains and plains had offered up until then. So far the immigrants had passed on into the mountains, but both John Smith and the Indians knew that someday this vanguard of white civilization was bound to stop and settle down upon the Middle Plains.

The Sioux and Northern Cheyennes were still commonly seen along the river, generally not bothering the immigration in accordance with the 1851 treaty and remaining away from Fort Laramie now that the soldiers, whom they did not trust, were there. Several trading firms operated along the trail below the fort: Bordeaux and Gerry, the American Fur Company, Ward and Guerrier, Drip's Trading Post, and others, all depending mostly on the Indian trade but also taking advantage of the needs of the emigrants. Francis Parkman, visiting the fort in 1846, listed the price of sugar at two dollars a cup, five-cent tobacco at $1.50, and bullets at 75¢ a pound.

John Smith still continued to trade during the winter months and work for Fitzpatrick during the summer, guiding the wagon trains of annuity goods into the Indian country, holding councils, and passing on the agent's advice and counsel on keeping the peace.

Fitzpatrick and Smith met the Cheyennes and Arapahoes near the ruins of old Fort St. Vrain, at the mouth of St. Vrain Creek on the South Platte, during the summer of 1852 and delivered $30,000 worth of goods to the tribes.[4] They did the same in the fall of 1853 for the purpose of distributing more annuity goods and also securing the signatures of the chiefs on the revised version of the Fort Laramie Treaty, in which Congress had reduced the length of annuity payments from fifteen to ten years.[5] It took over ten days for the runners to get all the

---

[4] Hafen, "First Indian Agency in Colorado," 53–62.

[5] Report of the Commissioner of Indian Affairs, 1853, 365–66. Report of Thomas Fitzpatrick, St. Louis, November 19, 1853.

bands in, but when this had been accomplished the agent had Smith read the new version of the treaty to the Indians and explain the amendments first to the head chiefs and then to the two nations in full council.

The chiefs—some of the original signers were now dead—signed the new version willingly, after which the goods, provisions, and ammunition were passed out to the various bands. By the time they had finished treating with the Indians, the nights were already becoming increasingly colder. With similar proceedings to accomplish with the Sioux at Fort Laramie, the two mountain men waved goodbye to the Indian bands as they departed for their final hunts of the season, their travois leaving trails of dust behind them, and then headed northward themselves along the South Platte.

At Fort Laramie they found the Sioux in a state of disturbance over recent troubles with the military which had resulted in several of their people being killed. But Fitzpatrick calmed their fears and secured their signatures to the new treaty, then rode off down the Platte road toward St. Louis. From there he wrote his annual report to the Commissioner of Indian Affairs, greatly concerned about the dark future of the Indians whom he expected to perish before the pending onslaught of whites onto the Indian lands.

This was the last time that John Smith or the Indians would ever see the famous mountain man, who would long be remembered as the most respected and best liked agent the Cheyennes would ever know. That winter while at Washington, Fitzpatrick developed pneumonia and died February 7, 1854.

Fitzpatrick was succeeded by Colonel John W. Whitfield, who arrived on the South Platte in July of 1854 with a trainload of annuity goods, finding there most of the

Arkansas and South Platte Cheyennes. The Northern Cheyennes, dissatisfied over the presence of troops on the North Platte, remained away, as did both the Northern and Southern Arapahoes, who were feuding over the killing of an Arapaho chieftain by one of the Northern bands.

Whitfield had come by the way of Bent's Fort where he met with Governor Merriweather of New Mexico, who had asked him to secure the release of some Mexican prisoners captured by the Cheyennes that spring. Whitfield convinced the Cheyennes to give up a white boy, originally from Iowa, and two Mexicans. Whitfield then journeyed on to Fort Laramie, meeting some twenty-five lodges of Sioux who were retreating from the Platte following a serious altercation between them and a Laramie soldier command.[6]

This trouble had occurred when a young West Point graduate named Lieutenant John L. Grattan, who had already displayed an extremely arrogant and belligerent attitude toward the Indians in general, took some troops out to look for an Indian who had killed an immigrant's cow which had wandered into his village. Finding the Sioux encampment east of the fort near Bordeaux's, Grattan marched his troops into the village and formed a line with his two howitzers aimed at the Indians.

Grattan's interpreter, Lucien August was drunk and transmitted the officer's arrogant attitude by informing the Indians that if they didn't cooperate "he would eat

---

[6] *Report of the Commissioner of Indian Affairs, 1854*, 92–93. When Whitfield resigned in 1855 he stated emphatically that, having barely escaped with his life for the past two years, ". . . permit me to say most explicitly that I could not again be induced to go amongst those Indians without a strong military escort or without a large quantity of guns and ammunition." Letters Received, Office of Indian Affairs, Upper Arkansas Agency, 1855–64. Though William Bent served as Whitfield's interpreter on the Little Blue in 1855, John Smith lists Whitfield as among those agents he served. *Massacre of Cheyenne Indians*, 11.

their hearts raw." A fight resulted, evidently with the troops firing first. After the soldiers had discharged their muskets, the Indians rushed in upon them, killing the entire twenty-eight men. The Sioux then robbed the trading house of Bordeaux and Chouteau and fled the vicinity. Bordeaux's account of the affair was verified by several of the frontiersmen in the vicinity, including John Smith.[7]

The massacre of Grattan led the government in Washington to approve punitive actions against the Indians, and during the late summer of 1855, General William S. Harney led an expedition out of Fort Leavenworth and up the Platte past Fort Kearny. On the Little Blue, just north of the Platte about halfway between Fort Kearny and Laramie, Harney attacked a large Sioux village, killing eighty-six Indians. Through the commander of Fort Laramie, Harney then demanded that the tribes all withdraw from the vicinity of the Platte road.

While Harney was out chastising the Indians, newly appointed Indian agent for the North Platte Thomas Twiss arrived at Fort Laramie in August of 1855 and immediately began attempts to separate the friendly bands of Cheyennes and Sioux from the hostile. A letter written by Twiss on October 15 indicates the important services rendered him by his two guide-interpreters, Antoine Iarvis and John Smith.

> I engaged on my arrival the services of two men who have been traders with the Indians for many years—one of them, Jno. Smith, has resided with the Cheyennes fifteen years; the other, Antoine Iarvis, with the Ogallalah & Brule band of Sioux twelve years—Both of these men were personally acquainted with the principal men of the respective bands, have done me good service, & given me assistance in the discharge of my duties, have encountered difficulties, and dangers that would have appalled

---

[7] Letters Received, Office of Indian Affairs, Upper Platte Agency, 1846–56. Letters August 29, 31, 1854, to Colonel Whitfield.

any other men who I have with me in the Agency—I have had
them on constant duty, sometimes riding as Expresses to collect
the Indians when no other white man could be hired on any
terms and then, after having gathered the Indians together, riding with me, in many instances, fifty miles in the capacity of
Interpreter . . . we remained in the saddle almost constantly
for 6 weeks.[8]

Twiss, a West Pointer from New York, was a man of
energy and determination, but he soon became involved
in some actions which were at least ill-advised and immediately antagonized just about everybody in the area. The
military, both Colonel William Hoffman at Laramie and
General Harney in winter quarters at Fort Pierre, considered Twiss to be a troublesome pacifist on Indian matters.
Sioux agent Colonel Alfred Vaughn was angered over
what he considered to be Twiss' meddling into Sioux affairs. The Indians, already unhappy, were complaining
that Twiss was cheating them on annuities.

But it was when Twiss, in early 1856, revoked the trading licenses of the local traders and virtually forbade them
from entering Fort Laramie that he stirred up a hornet's
nest.[9] Immediately Ward and Guerrier wrote a stinging
letter to Hoffman, complaining that Twiss was an "unprincipled individual" who was robbing them of their
livelihood and forcing them to "endure the rigors of a
very severe winter in skin lodges."[10] They further claimed
that he was defrauding the government by using the Indian annuity goods for his own private use and, besides

---

[8] Letters Received, Office of Indian Affairs, Central Superintendency, 1852–80.
Thomas Twiss to Colonel Cummings, Fort Laramie, October 15, 1855.

[9] Letters Received, Office of Indian Affairs, Upper Platte Agency, 1846–56, National Archives, Thomas Twiss to traders Ward and Guerrier, I. Bisenette, Beauvais,
Bordeau, Richard and Simenno, January 31, 1856.

[10] *Ibid.*, Ward and Guerrier to Colonel Hoffman, Fort Laramie, February 7,
1856.

offering them competition in the trade of furs, had purchased a young Sioux squaw with them. This was supported by a statement by Antoine Iarvis.

In late February, Agent Vaughn arrived at Laramie and took sworn affidavits from all the traders there. William Guerrier testified that once he went into Twiss' lodge and saw two packs of buffalo robes (ten robes to the pack) and commented to his old friend, John Smith, that it looked as though the agent "was beginning to make his packs." According to Guerrier, Smith replied, "Yes, he was, and that he was breaking his neck fast."[11]

Similar statements were made under oath by Guerrier's partner, Seth Ward, by John Richard, and by others. On March 3, Smith was interrogated under oath by Colonel Vaughn and in sworn testimony stated that Twiss had used Indian goods for the subsistence of himself and his employees through the winter, Smith included, and that Twiss had given disproportionate amounts of goods to the chiefs, principally the Sioux chief, Standing Elk, and had received Standing Elk's daughter in return.[12]

Harney ordered Hoffman to restrict Twiss in connection with the Cheyennes and Arapahoes and to allow him to have nothing at all to do with the Sioux. Twiss appealed to Commissioner Manypenny in Washington, claiming a conspiracy by the traders and military to break the agency, then took a vacation to the East for a visit

---

[11] *Ibid.*, Affadavit by William Guerrier, February 27, 1856.

[12] Records of War Department, Office of Adjutant General, Letters Received, 1855–59. Berthrong Collection, Oklahoma University Division of Manuscripts. Bvt. Brig. General Harney to Col. S. Cooper, March 23, 1856, enclosing copy of inquiries made to John S. Smith, Interpreter, at Fort Pierre. In November, 1858, while he was at Cherry Creek, Smith was asked to forward a copy of the interrogations of Colonel Vaughn to Washington. Smith stated: "Testimony of this nature is abundant, and the tribes themselves, realize the full truth of it." Letters Received, Upper Platte Agency, 1857–62.

with his family in Troy. He returned to Bissonette's trading house near Laramie in July, and in August he was reinstated by Harney on orders from Washington.

During Twiss' absence, John Smith accompanied Agent Vaughn and Iarvis to Fort Pierre where on March 1-5, 1856, they attended a big council between General Harney and the Sioux.[13]

During the summer of 1856, more trouble developed between the Indians and the Fort Laramie military, this time with the Cheyennes over four stray horses which the Indians had picked up on the prairie and which Hoffman demanded they hand over. Three horses were brought in by Cheyenne braves, but the fourth was held on to by Little Wolf, who claimed that it had been found at another time and another place.[14]

Dissatisfied, Hoffman ordered the three placed under arrest. One of them broke away from his guard and escaped while another was killed in the attempt. The Cheyenne band fled, leaving behind their lodges and effects, which were burned by the troops. The Indians came across an old trapper named Ganier and killed him. In May Cheyenne chief Dull Knife visited Fort Laramie, saying that the Cheyennes desired peace. But in June a war party of Cheyennes and Arapahoes hit an emigrant train on the Little Blue in eastern Kansas, killing one man. The party went on into Fort Kearny where the commanding officer, Captain H. W. Wharton, took three of the group hostage, only to have them escape with one badly wounded.

---

[13] Letters Received, Office of Indian Affairs, Upper Platte Agency, 1846-56, National Archives, Account of Fort Pierre Council, March 12, 1856. The Sioux turned down Twiss' suggestion that Smith be taken to Fort Pierre as their interpreter on the grounds that he did not know their language well enough. Hoffman to Pleasonton, Fort Laramie, Feb. 12, 1856.

[14] Letters Sent, Fort Laramie, Hoffman to Capt. H. Heth, May 24, 1856.

On July 28, Hoffman dispatched John Smith and an officer from Laramie to Kearny to search for five deserters and to pick up Cheyenne news there and on the road.[15] The Cheyenne news soon became abundant. In August some Cheyenne hot-bloods stopped a mail wagon and wounded the driver near Kearny. Wharton sent out Captain George Stewart with forty-one mounted troops. Stewart found a Cheyenne camp near Grand Island on the Platte, struck it, and killed several Indians. This, in turn, touched off a Cheyenne retaliatory raid all along the Platte road, against wagon trains and settlements, with wholesale killing, scalping, and prisoners being taken. One woman was killed and another was captured from a Mormon train, while a four-year-old boy was taken from another.

Upon his return, Twiss had tried to get Hoffman to release the Cheyenne prisoner at Laramie to no avail. With John Smith interpreting, Twiss held two days of councils with the Cheyenne chiefs at Fort Laramie.[16] He admonished the chief Old Soldier and others for the depredations they had committed and suggested that a trade be made—the Cheyenne prisoner for the woman and boy. On the second day, the boy was brought in, but Twiss was told that the woman had escaped and had been picked up by a topographical party which happened to be near the Cheyenne village on the Republican River at the time.

Twiss convinced the chiefs that the Cheyennes should follow a course of peace and withdraw from the Platte

[15] Records of War Department, Fort Laramie, Berthrong Collection, Oklahoma University Division of Manuscripts. Major Hoffman, Fort Laramie, to Captain Wharton, Fort Kearny, July 28, 1856.

[16] Alban W. Hoopes, "Thomas S. Twiss, Indian Agent on the Upper Platte, 1855–1861," *Mississippi Valley Historical Review*, XX, 1933–34 353–64. Letters Received, Upper Platte Agency, 1857–62. Twiss to Denver, Rawhide Creek, August 18, 1857.

road, and there can be little doubt that John was a persuasive force for the agent. In speaking of the unscrupulous traders in the region, a theme that Fitzpatrick stressed many times, Twiss obviously had Smith among those in mind when he wrote:

> But these rare examples of high-minded and honorable men residing the Indian country do not destroy the force of my argument. They came to the country when young, and remain here, far from the circles of civilization, by the force of habit and inclination, and the interests of the Indian trade in which they are engaged.[17]

Despite his earlier indiscretions, Twiss' policy of keeping the peace with the Indians was far more realistic than that of the military, who could offer the emigration virtually no protection whatsoever once a punitive strike had been made against the tribes. The Cheyennes had remained quiet following the Laramie conference, but Harney and others were still convinced that it was necessary to punish the Indians. Accordingly, Colonel E. V. Sumner was given the signal for an expedition against the Cheyennes during the summer of 1857.

Directing one column of troops under Major John Sedgwick to move from Fort Leavenworth up the Arkansas route to Bent's Fort and then along the mountains to Fort St. Vrain, Sumner himself led a second column to Fort Laramie and then up the South Platte to St. Vrain Creek where he united with Sedgwick. On July 17, Hoffman at Laramie sent Elbridge Gerry out to join Sumner as a guide and interpreter.[18]

---

[17] *Commissioner of Indian Affairs, 1856,* 639.

[18] Letters Sent, Fort Laramie, Bvt. Col. W. Hoffman to Col. E. V. Sumner, Fort Laramie, July 7, 1857. Gerry took another man with him, but whether or not it might have been John Smith the incomplete records of the expedition do not reveal. Smith once told George Bent that "Colonel Sumner and his officers were mean to all the Indians, even they were down on old timers also." George Bent Letters, Feb. 19, 1913.

Already with Sumner was Smith's old friend, Jim Bridger, who had recently been displaced from his Green River trading post by the Mormons.[19] Along also was the frontier-famous Delaware chief, Fall Leaf.

From St. Vrain, Sumner advanced eastward with a command of over 400 troops and four mountain howitzers. On July 29, 1857, he found the Cheyennes on the Solomon River, fully bonneted and painted, drawn up in battle array and ready to fight. They had been primed by their medicine man who had told them that by dipping their hands in a nearby lake they could make the soldiers' bullets fall harmlessly from their guns.

It was one of the few classic confrontations of U.S. troops and Plains Indians in the history of the West. Sumner, by luck or otherwise, chose to charge the Cheyenne line of warriors with sabers instead of guns. This unexpected strategy destroyed the Cheyenne readiness to fight and quickly turned the battle into a rout. Sumner claimed thirty warriors were killed, while losing only two men himself. Among the wounded was Lieutenant J. E. B. Stuart, who was hit in the chest with a ball from an old Allen's revolver dated 1837. Stuart and the other wounded were sent in to Fort Kearny while Sumner, after destroying the Cheyennes' village and their winter meat supply, followed the fleeing Indians southward toward the Arkansas River.

While at the Cimarron Crossing, Sumner learned that a new Cheyenne and Arapaho Agent, Robert C. Miller, was at Bent's Fort with a train load of annuity goods. Sumner marched to the fort and dumped the goods into the river.

Whether Smith played any part in this affair is not known. He was still at Fort Laramie in early September,

[19] *New York Tribune*, Sept. 10, 1857.

1857, when an army expedition passed by on its way to Utah to put down the Mormon rebellion. Captain John Phelps wrote in his diary on September 7: "We took a guide at Fort Laramie for the purpose of disclosing to us the best grazing possible. His name is John S. Smith and he has been in this region and on the plains as a fur trader for a great many years. But he can certainly do more at talking than in finding grass."[20]

Sumner had driven the Cheyennes away from the Platte to the Arkansas, shifting both their trading operation and annuity distribution there. Thus when Miller arrived on the Arkansas during the summer of 1858, he secured the services of William Bent as interpreter and dispensed the goods to the tribes at Pawnee Fork.[21] Sumner's expedition had encountered a small group of Missouri gold seekers while in Colorado; also Fall Leaf had taken back to Kansas some gold nuggets which he had found in the South Platte country.

These, and other sources which were even then telling the world of the possibility of gold in the mountains, were setting the stage for a dramatic upheaval in the situation of the Western Plains and in the life of John Smith.

---

[20] L. R. and A. W. Hafen *The Utah Expedition, 1857–1858, Far West and Rockies Series.* VIII, (Glendale, Calif: The Arthur H. Clark Co., 1958), 125.

[21] *Commissioner of Indian Affairs, 1857*, 144–48.

6

On the South Platte

Later in that year 1856 I came across this way with John S. Smith, an old trapper and "squaw man." Together we built a little cabin about where Twelfth and Wazee Streets now are. This, I believe, was the first house built on the present site of Denver. . . Captain Charles Christy.[1]

Few locations, indeed, surpassed the one which John Smith used to conduct his trading operations during the 1850s. Here Cherry Creek meandered out of the southeast and made its juncture with the South Platte, while not far below, the larger Clear Creek cut its way through the Rockies. The mountains, whose snow-capped peaks gleamed above the purplish foothills, stood like a giant barrier which had been thrown across the continent. Along it ran the South Platte, a clear-flowing, sand-bottomed stream whose waters began the long voyage to join the North Platte, then the Missouri, the Mississippi, and eventually emptied into the Gulf of Mexico.

As a trading location, the South Platte was choice, striking a mid-point between the divisions of the Cheyenne and the Arapaho bands, as well as those of the Sioux, the Crow, and other tribes from the Sweetwater and Green rivers who were occasional visitors to Smith's trading lodge. Moreover, the South Platte region was well

---

[1] "The Personal Memoirs of Captain Charles Christy," as narrated by himself. *The Trail*, I (June 1908), 14. Cited in Mumey, *Early Settlements*, 33.

away from the migratory roads of the white man; the water, grass, and game were still bountiful along the eastern plateau of the Colorado Rockies. It was an excellent wintering ground for the Cheyennes, who had only to move eastward along the Smoky Hill, Republican, Beaver, or Solomon rivers of western Kansas for their spring, summer, and fall buffalo hunts.

Fitzpatrick himself in 1853 described the "sheltered valleys, mild temperatures, large growths of timber, and an immense water power," which "together with an abundance of small game, render it a favorite resort of the Indian during the winter months, and enable them to subsist their animals in the severest seasons."[2]

The region had long been popular as a trapping and trading area. Jean Champlain and Ezekial Williams had trapped and hunted here in 1811, as had A. P. Chouteau, Julius DeMunn, and Josephy Philibert in 1815, and William Becknell, William Heddest, and Antoine Robidioux in 1824. Fort Vasquez had been established at the mouth of Clear Creek in 1832 by Vasquez and Sublette, and abandoned around 1840. In 1836 or 1837, Lieutenant Lupton, who had explored this region with Dodge in 1835 and liked it, also built Fort Lancaster (or Lupton), while twelve miles above at the mouth of St. Vrain Creek, where the South Platte turned from a northerly to an easterly flow, Bent and St. Vrain had established Fort St. Vrain in 1837 or 1838.[3] Another old trapper's fort was mentioned by early visitors to the region.

As a natural avenue for traffic along the east side of the mountains, the area saw the passage of early explorers—

---

[2] *Commissioner of Indian Affairs, 1853*, 365–66.

[3] On December 22, 1856, Twiss wrote that "St. Vrain's on the South Fork of the Platte has been deserted for five years." Letters Received, Upper Platte Agency, 1857–62.

Mallet in 1739, Long in 1819, Pattie and Young in 1826, Dodge in 1835, Fremont in 1843–44, and others—while visitors such as Dr. F.A. Wislizenus in 1839 and Rufus Sage in 1842 provided interesting accounts of those days when the fur trade flourished along the South Platte.

Though John Smith evades mention in these frontier narratives, there can be little doubt but that he played an active role in the Fort St. Vrain saga, since Bent and St. Vrain were his employers and the Cheyennes were known to hang close to the region. Sage mentions meeting a camp of Bent and St. Vrain men on a small island of the South Platte in 1842, while historian Hafen believed that John Smith must have been with a Blackfoot camp on Cherry Creek in September of that same year.[4] Wislizenus had found Fitzpatrick at Fort Vasquez in 1839, indicating that Smith and Fitzpatrick crossed trails on numerous occasions during the early trading days.

But for one reason or another, organized trading operation on the South Platte had ceased by the mid-1840's, St. Vrain being abandoned and in ruins when Francis Parkman visited it in 1846, leaving a vacuum of trading potential for John Smith, whose activities as a trader in the region are evidenced by Gerry's account books. An entry dated April 2, 1853, lists the goods supplied to Smith and the robe price paid by him to Gerry: vermillion, two robes; scarlet, two robes; sugar, one robe; hickory shirts, one robe; red blanket, two robes; blue blanket, two robes; tobacco, two robes; blue drill, two robes; looking glass and cup, one robe; powder and bullets, one robe; beads, two robes; calico, one-half robe.[5]

The account books show that Smith continued these

---

[4] Rufus Sage, *His Letters and Papers, 1836–1847, Far West and Rockies Series,* v. LeRoy R. and Ann W. Hafen., eds., (Glendale: The Arthur H. Clark Co., 1956), 70.

[5] Gerry Account Books, Colorado Historical Society, Book 1.

trading operations through the winter of 1857–58. A sizable outfit is listed in his name on December 14, 1857, for trade on the South Fork of the Platte. The goods listed as received by Smith from Gerry and Bordeau totaled $4,159.73 and included all the standard trade items: blankets, cloths, bed ticking, muslin, hickory and red flannel shirts, pants, brass kettles, wire, mirrors, Chinese vermillion, bean seed beads, barley corn beads, awls, hawk bells, tin pans, tin cups, tin plates, tea kettles, ebony knives, coca knives, coffee mills, combs, thread, brass buttons and rings, hoes, half axes, large axes, ax handles, food staples, tobacco, soap, candy, raisins, kegs of powder, percussion caps, lead balls, and other items—and it also listed twenty-one head of cattle, wagons, log cabins, yokes with bows, and wages paid men and transportation.[6]

These last items may indicate that the Indian trade was not all that was on Smith's mind. Smiley, in his *History of Denver*, claims that during the summer of 1857 John Smith had started a settlement within the present city limits of Denver known as the "Mexican Diggin's" or "Spanish Diggin's" about three miles up the South Platte from the mouth of Cherry Creek. Smith is said to have employed a company of Mexicans in placer mining for gold and worked it until the spring of 1858 when the gold was exhausted, after which time the settlement disappeared.[7]

It is certain that Smith knew about the potential for mineral wealth held by the mountains he had roamed so often. If Tom Fitzpatrick knew, then John Smith knew, and in one of his reports the Indian agent had written that

---

[6] Gerry Account Books, Book 2.

[7] Jerome C. Smiley, *History of Denver* (Denver: Times-Sun Publishing Co., 1901), 182–89.

"Indications of mineral wealth likewise abound in the sands of the water courses, and the gorges and canons from which they issue." In fact, Fitzpatrick predicted with great historical accuracy that "should public attention ever be strongly directed to this section of our territory . . . the inducements which it holds out will soon people it with thousands of citizens, and cause it to rise speedily into a flourishing mountain State."[8]

Reports of gold in Colorado had been circulating for a long time. In 1765 a Spaniard named Juan Rivera returned to Santa Fe with ore samples taken from the Colorado mountains. Zebulon Pike in 1807 met American James Purcell and was told of gold discoveries. In 1823 James Cockrell found silver in the region, and in 1827 led a party of Missourians to the site of present Trinidad, Colorado. In 1833 the Estes party found a good placer bar near Cherry Creek but left because of Indians. Sage in 1843 met three men in southeast Colorado with two pack mules laden with gold and silver. A trapper named Williams claimed to have penetrated South Park in 1848 and discovered gold, as did John Orlbert in 1851. William Gilpin, an early western explorer and the first territorial governor of Colorado, wrote of stories of gold in the Rockies as early as 1848, the same year that some of the Bent children reportedly found some small nuggets on Crow Creek when returning from Fort Bridger.

Two parties of Cherokee Indians on their way from Georgia to the California gold fields in 1849 and 1850 found "color" on the South Platte near the mouth of Cherry Creek, eventually bringing the word back to Georgia where Green Russell, who was married into the tribe, heard the stories. Fall Leaf, Sumner's guide, re-

---

[8] *Commissioner of Indian Affairs, 1853*, 366.

turned from the Cheyenne expedition with some gold nuggets tied up in a rag, claiming he had found them on a rock when drinking from a small stream emptying into the South Platte. He showed the nuggets about in Lawrence, stirring interest there in a prospecting expedition to the region.

A party of Missourians was encountered by Sumner, also, and from them he heard reports of gold. George Simpson, with a government supply train, found gold dust on Cherry Creek in May of 1858. Other accounts tell of Bissonette and other traders from the Laramie area visiting the Pike's Peak area to prospect for gold, and there were undoubtedly many other gold-seeking ventures made into the region which were never recorded. But it was John Simpson Smith who made the first serious attempt to conduct mining operations on the South Platte.

The Gerry books show that on June 16, 1858, Smith's returns to the trading post at Laramie included buffalo robes, bear skins, wolf skins, badger skins, wild cat skins, parfleche, caberas, buckskins, horses, and mules as well as unsold blankets, cloth, beads, coffee, sugar, etc. He was outfitted again on July 7 for trade on the South Platte and the Arkansas.[9]

On June 24, while Smith was at Fort Laramie, the Green Russell gold rush party, consisting of 104 men, arrived at the conflux of Cherry Creek and the South Platte and began panning up and down the river beds for signs of gold. A month later, on July 25, most of the group was discouraged at the lack of success and returned to Kansas, but thirteen of them continued prospecting up the South Platte some eighty miles with Russell. When they returned to their Cherry Creek camp the prospec-

---

[9] Gerry Account Books, Book 2.

tors were greeted by ". . . an old mountaineer by the name of Smith, who had not seen any white men for about six weeks."[10]

John Smith was a big help to the Russell men, giving freely of his extensive knowledge of the country until they left in August to prospect into Wyoming and Utah. When they returned again they found that Smith had been joined by several other frontiersmen and their Indian families, as well as by another gold rush group, the Lawrence Party. Still helpful, Smith assisted in building a two-room log house on the banks of the Platte.[11] And when the third gold rush group, the Leavenworth-Lecompton Party, arrived in November, they were shown frontier hospitality by Smith and the other mountain men who "had warm lodges and made us feel comfortable and homelike."[12]

Though there is some confusion on the point, it seems apparent that a log cabin built by Smith already stood when the first goldseekers arrived. One man wrote home from Cherry Creek on November 8, 1858, that: "We are comfortably fixed; have a good cabin that was built some years ago by some trader, and we have use of it until spring."[13]

Wharton, in his *History of Denver*, agrees that Smith did build the first house on the site of Denver, but gives 1857 as the date, while the Colorado *Gazetteer* for 1871 states that "The first rude trapper's hut built in Colorado occupied a site within the present limits of Denver, and

[10] Hafen, LeRoy R., ed., *Pike's Peak Guidebooks of 1859, Southwest Historical Series*, vol. IV, (Glendale, Calif: The Arthur H. Clark Co., 1941), 206–7. Letter, William McKimens, Auraria City, November 11, 1858.   [11] *Ibid.*, 76–77.

[12] Nolie Mumey, *History of the Early Settlements of Denver* (Glendale, Calif: The Arthur H. Clark Co., 1942), 8.

[13] *Leavenworth Times*, December 18, 1858. As cited in LeRoy R. Hafen ed., *Colorado Gold Rush, Southwest Historical Series*, vol. X, (Glendale, Calif: The Arthur H. Clark Co., 1941), 159.

was occupied by one of the omnipresent and never-dying Smith family. It was built in the fall of 1857."[14]

Letters from Cherry Creek indicate that Smith was a big help to the newcomers in many ways. He assisted with the construction of cabins, gave them invaluable information concerning the geography and wild life of the land, and was undoubtedly of considerable benefit to them on the simple matters of survival in the wilderness. And the men of the Lawrence party quickly realized another important function that Smith could serve.

Anxious to beat out the other gold rush groups in founding a town organization, the Lawrence men laid out Montana City on the east side of the Platte, soon turning to another site on the east side of Cherry Creek. On September 24, 1858, some seven men of the Lawrence group met in the lodge of William McGaa, a squawman friend of Smith's with McGaa and Smith, and organized the St. Charles Town Association, electing Smith as their treasurer.[15] As one gold rushee admitted: "We took Jack McGaa and John Smith into the Company as they were squawmen and thought they might be of some benefit to us in holding the land for town purposes."[16] Leaving Smith, McGaa and Charles Nichols to hold their claims, the group returned to Kansas Territory to promote their new town. The three men were to build cabins on each half section, and McGaa claims they did this: ". . . houses or cabins were built by Jno. Smith and William McGaa in the fall of 1859 and occupied by Smith and McGaa."[17]

---

[14] *Colorado Resorts and Attractions to the Pleasure-Seeker, Tourist and Invalid, 1873,* 7. Quoting the *Colorado Gazetteer* for 1871.

[15] Mumey, *Early Settlements,* 58.

[16] "The Lawrence Party of Pike's Peakers and the Founding of St. Charles," *Colorado Magazine,* X (September 1953), 195–96.

[17] William McGaa, "A Statement Regarding the Formation of the St. Charles and Denver Town Companies," *Colorado Magazine,* XXII (May 1945), 125–29.

DENVER CITY

An 1858 view of the new settlement at the conflux of Cherry Creek and the South Platte. The frontiersman in the foreground might well be John Smith, who built the first cabin there in 1856 and greeted the arrival of the first gold rush party.

Courtesy, State Historical Society of Colorado

The Georgia group, concerned that they might well get left out of a good thing, quickly organized the Auraria Town Company, and on October 29 they purchased preemptory rights held by John Smith to the area on the west side of Cherry Creek for a nominal consideration.[18] Eight cabins had already been constructed on the site.

Among the Leavenworth-Lecompton group was a tall, good-looking young adventurer from Pennsylvania named Edward Wynkoop, who had been appointed as Sheriff of Arapahoe County, Kansas, which then encompassed the gold rush area. Wynkoop and John Smith were destined to ride many trails together in the days ahead.

Sizing the situation quickly, the Leavenworth-Lecompton men, headed by General William Larimer, plied McGaa, who was supposedly holding the townsite claim for the St. Charles group, with whiskey and jumped the claim on the grounds that it had been abandoned. McGaa later admitted to the acceptance of "ardent spirits" but claimed also that the men threatened him, "endangering the life of myself and family."[19]

Smith and McGaa were accorded the ferry privilege by the Auraria Town Company, consisting of 320 acres known as the McGaa and Smith Ferry Landing. McGaa sold out his interest, and it is to be assumed that John Smith did likewise.

Several meetings were held in November to form a new town company, which was at first called Golden City but was changed to Denver City upon Wynkoop's suggestion that it be named so in honor of Governor Denver of Kansas. John Smith was one of the original forty-two members of the Denver City Town Company, a charter for which was obtained following a heroic trip by Wynkoop and A. B. Steinberger back to Kansas. The trip, made by

---

[18] Mumey, *Early Settlements*, 53.   [19] McGaa, "A Statement."

way of the Platte Trail and Omaha, took a month, through sub-zero weather, and involved an icy river crossing during which Wynkoop fell through the ice and froze his feet.

A street in the new township was justly named for Wynkoop. Judge H. P. A. Smith, of the Leavenworth-Lecompton party, took the Smith honors on street names, so another of them was named "Wapoola" for John Smith's squaw.[20]

Letters from the new settlement give some interesting clues as to Smith's activities during this time. A letter appearing in the *Lawrence Republican* on October 21, 1858, stated that "A half-breed Cheyenne boy, John Smith by name, son of John S. Smith, well known as an old Indian trader, had been at work about two weeks . . . and had made fourteen dollars per week with his pan, shovel, and pick, carrying his dirt from ten to twenty rods."[21] Another, written on December 17th, lists John Smith as a member of the temperance society of the church in Auraria.[22] A description of an early church service involving Smith was penned by young William Larimer: "It was a morning service. The congregation was small, although Mr. Fisher (the preacher) and father went around and invited everybody to attend. There were no church bells to ring, no pews to sit in. But seated on the buffalo robes spread on the ground, with the Jones and Smith squaws present (there were no other ladies) Fisher, father, myself and perhaps six or eight others held the first religious service ever held in this country . . . At the other end of the cabin could be heard the jingle of money where gambling was in progress at the same time."[23]

[20] Mumey, *Early Settlements*, Map enclosure.

[21] Hafen, ed. *Colorado Gold Rush*, 93.   [22] *Ibid.*, 186.

[23] LeRoy R. Hafen and Ann W. Hafen, *Colorado, A Story of the State and Its People* (Denver: Old West Publishing Co., 1944) 161–62.

It was during these days in infant Denver that John Smith was dubbed "Uncle John" by the miners. Others, with frontier humor, claimed they wished to be "historically accurate" and dubbed Smith's Cheyenne wife "Pocohantas."

At Christmas season that first year of the gold rush, the whites and the Indians still felt friendly enough to interassociate. Arapahoe chiefs Left Hand and Little Raven brought their bands in to the log-house and lodge settlement on the banks of the South Platte for a celebration. They especially wished to enjoy a favorite pastime of horse racing, at which "they could be beat but cannot be backed out." The Arapahoes challenged the Americans with a pony on which they were willing to bet 150 other ponies at a quarter mile. They also had a Mexican mule which they were willing to put up against any other trotting mule at the same risk. The whites had no mules that could trot, but someone knew of one in Westport which they planned to bring out.

A huge feast was held in Auraria for some five hundred of the Arapahoes, serving roast oxen, bread, coffee, and dried apples. The miners were amazed to hear Little Raven talk English, see him eat with a knife and fork, and smoke cigars just like a civilized man. Celebrations of this nature were accompanied with considerable drinking, and on a similar occasion later some of the rougher element in infant Denver invaded an Arapahoe camp and attacked and raped some of the Indian women. It was, in fact, such goings-on that brought an abrupt end to John Smith's flirtation with civilized society. A letter written from Denver City on January 7, 1859, tells the story well:

> We have preaching here every Sunday morning by an "old gentleman miner," of the Methodist race, horse racing after preaching, gambling after speeches, dancing after gambling, and to wind up the grand performance of the Sabbath, after the

dance our beloved and most respected friend, the original John S. Smith breaks his squaw's back with a creepy, or a three legged stool, for daring without his permission to trip the light fantastic toe. The original John S. Smith has just been served notice to leave this town in four days; his conduct had been such of late that the mining community will stand it no longer. His squaw is suffering severely from the effects of the said creepy. The original John S. goes into exile alone, among the Arapahoes, there to recruit his almost shattered fortunes.[24]

Smith left Denver along with the Arapahoes, more than likely feeling unappreciated and certainly misunderstood over the accepted custom of beating his squaw. Along with some of his Indian trader friends he relocated at Miraville City, forty miles north of Denver on Big Thompson Creek where he was listed in the 1860 census of western Nebraska. From there he moved a bit further north to the Cache la Poudre branch of the South Platte. The *Rocky Mountain News* of May 2, 1860, reported that Smith had built a road from his ranch to the upper crossing of the Platte.[25]

The Gerry account books show that Smith brought returns into Fort Laramie on December 26, 1858, and that he continued to trade for Gerry into 1861.[26] But the news of gold in Colorado and the ensuing stampede of whites to Pike's peak and Cherry Creek had caused waves in Washington that would backwash to Colorado and once again pull John Smith back to the Arkansas River.

It had become apparent to the government that the horde of illegal trespassers on the lands of the Cheyennes and Arapahoes would somehow have to be legitimatized, just as the Indians needed to be removed from any interference with traffic to and from the gold fields. The Indi-

---

[24] Hafen, *Colorado Gold Rush*, 207–08. Letter from John W. Jones, Denver City, January 7, 1859.

[25] Ann W. Hafen, "John Simpson Smith," 338.

[26] Gerry Account Books, No. 2.

ans were concerned about the whites taking over their best hunting and wintering grounds, and William Bent, now serving as their agent, was having a hard time keeping them quiet. The tribes felt, too, that a new treaty should be made, and in the fall of 1860 Commissioner of Indian Affairs A. B. Greenwood himself made a trip from Washington to treat with the Indians.[27] The site was the new fort which Bent had constructed in 1853 on the rock bluff which overlooked the Arkansas River just below the Big Timbers.

The new treaty effort coincided with another major development on the Arkansas, the purchase of Bent's New Fort by the War Department and the construction of Fort Wise at the Big Timbers. Major Sedgwick and Lieutenant J. E. B. Stuart were there, as were many frontier notables, including John Smith, Colonel Albert G. Boone, who had recently founded Booneville just up the river from Bent's old fort, Charlie Autobees, John Hatcher, Dick Wootton, William Bent, and others.[28]

Smith, who had been assigned to the treaty council as the official interpreter once more, arrived at the meeting with a new Cheyenne wife, Zerepta, and a second baby son, named William Gilpin Smith. He was immediately assigned the chore of riding out to round up the principal chiefs of the Cheyennes and Arapahoes and bring them in to the council. He arrived back at Fort Wise in mid-September, 1860, with Cheyenne chiefs Black Kettle, White Antelope, Lean Bear, and Little Wolf in tow.

Commissioner of Indian Affairs A. B. Greenwood, meanwhile, had arrived at the Big Timbers to conduct the

---

[27] *Commissioner of Indian Affairs, 1860*, 452–54.

[28] Stan Hoig, *The Sand Creek Massacre* (Norman: University of Oklahoma Press, 1961), 8–17.

treaty personally, bringing with him thirteen wagons of goods for treating the Indians. Meeting with the chiefs, he commended them through Smith for remaining peaceful while other tribes, such as the Kiowas and Comanches, had been hostile. Because of their good conduct, he said, the Great Father wished to reward them and proceeded to outline details of an agreement which would reduce their lands from the Arkansas to the Platte to a small, game-barren area along the Arkansas River above Bent's old place.

In return for this, the government would pay them the sum of $30,000 a year for fifteen years with which they could purchase stock and agricultural implements, build storehouse, fence land, and break soil for planting. Additionally, they would be supplied with a sawmill, one or more repair shops, dwelling houses, and men to help them such as millers, farmers, mechanics, and interpreters. Each Indian was to receive forty acres of land, with timber and water where possible. An attempt by Denver business interests to be allowed the right to enter city and town lots on the reservation at $1.25 was struck out by Congress.[29]

This was all explained to the chiefs by Smith, and the chiefs appeared to have a clear understanding of the treaty terms. But while they were themselves agreeable to the treaty, they said they would have to put the matter to a vote of the entire tribe. Anxious to return to Washington, Greenwood hurriedly passed out the presents to the chiefs and headed east, turning the affair over to F. B. Culver. William Bent, perhaps dissatisfied over the terms of the treaty, knowing that the Indians were by no means ready to settle down to a permanent reserve, resigned his

[29] C. J. Kappler, ed., *Indian Affairs*, II, 807–11.

commission. He was replaced by Colonel Boone, who was well-liked by the Indians.[30]

It was February before Boone returned from Washington with the treaty papers. On February 18, 1861, Boone and Smith met with the Cheyenne and Arapaho chiefs and secured their signatures on the treaty: Little Raven, Storm, Shave-Head, and Big Mouth signing for the Arapahoes, and Black Kettle, White Antelope, Lean Bear, and Left Hand for the Cheyennes.[31] A postscript to the Treaty of Fort Wise awarded 640 acres of choice land in the Arkansas Valley to half-bloods Jack Smith and Robert Bent.

After all the treaty arrangements had been completed, Agent Boone on March 6, 1861, recognized Smith's services in a report to the Superintendent of Indian Affairs at St. Louis:

> Sir, on my arrival here previous to the Treaty with the Arappahos and Cheyennes I employed John S. Smith as U.S. Interpreter and he having given entire satisfaction to both the Indians and myself and during that time having deported himself properly I respectfully recommend him for the permanent Interpreter, and in as much as he speaks both the Arappaho and Cheyenne as well as Kiaway and Comanch and having readily yielded to the wish of the Agent to attend the treaty and having made considerable sacrifice by leaving his Ranch and Stock to go to waist, that he may have his salary raised so as to fully compensate him for the same.[32]

John Smith now made his home at the fort, which, with the outbreak of the Civil War in the spring of 1861, was renamed Fort Lyon. He still conducted trade with the

---

[30] *The Western Mountaineer*, October 4, 1860. Boone, Daniel's grandson who had helped to explore the West in his earlier days, founded Booneville upriver from Bent's place. He came West first in 1826 as a bookkeeper for a fur-trading expedition.

[31] There were two Left Hands during this period. One was an Arapaho chief. This Left Hand was a Cheyenne.

[32] Office of Indian Affairs, National Archives.

FORT LYON, COLORADO TERRITORY, 1864

John Simpson Smith made the fort his home during the years of the Civil War. An original structure was built by William Bent in this vicinity in 1853. Called Bent's New Fort, the site was taken by the Army in 1861 and Fort Wise was constructed. It was here that the Cheyenne and Arapaho signed a treaty on February 18, 1861. In the spring of that year, the fort was renamed Fort Lyon, following commencement of hostilities between the states.

Courtesy, Denver Public Library Western Collection

tribes, as well as working as interpreter and scout for the new agency and for the Fort Lyon military. Also living at the fort was a Lieutenant Sanford of the First Colorado Regiment of Volunteers and his young wife. During her stay there, Mrs. Sanford became acquainted with Smith, Zerepta, and little William Gilpin.[33]

The Smiths, who lived "quite civilized" according to Mrs. Sanford's diary, were visited one day by the Sanfords. During the visit, John Smith expressed his wish to present Mrs. Sanford with a pair of moccasins which Zerepta made and sold for five dollars a pair. It would have been a simple matter for him to take the moccasins and give them to Mrs. Sanford. Instead Smith gave a five-dollar gold piece to the Lieutenant and asked that he buy the footwear from Zerepta. The Indian woman was extremely pleased with the sale and happily returned the five-dollar gold piece to her husband.

In March, 1861, the Colorado Volunteers, stationed principally in Denver, received an urgent call for help from the Union forces in New Mexico who were being threatened by a Texas Confederate army advancing northward along the Rio Grande. Evacuation of Fort Lyon civilians to Denver was begun immediately. Mrs. Sanford and the Lieutenant were offered a ride by Smith in his wagon, and at night on the trail they were provided a place to sleep in the bed of the wagon while Smith, Zerepta, and little "Governor" Gilpin slept on the ground beneath the wagon.

While en route to Denver, the main force of the Colorado First Regiment was met as it made its heroic march toward Fort Union. Lieutenant Sanford joined the regi-

[33] Albert B. Sanford (ed.), "Life at Camp Weld and Fort Lyon in 1861–62, An Extract from the Diary of Mrs. Byron N. Sanford," *Colorado Magazine*, VII (May 1930), 135–37.

ment, while John Smith was asked to return to Fort Lyon with his wagon to pick up military baggage as the troops hurried on southward toward Raton Pass and Fort Union, from whence they would ultimately march for their great victory over the Texans at La Glorieta Pass in New Mexico.

The ensuing war years were spent by Smith mostly at Fort Lyon, assisting both the Indian Bureau and the Fort Lyon military in their dealing with the Indians. Though some weak efforts were made by the government to construct a couple of buildings on the site of the new agency and a field of corn was planted, the terms of the Treaty of Fort Wise were destined never to be put into effect. The Cheyennes and Arapahoes continued to employ the buffalo range of Western Kansas as their hunting grounds, coming into Forts Lyon and Larned, which had been established on the Pawnee Fork in 1859, to ask for their annuities which their tribes desperately needed. They received more promise than substance.

Meanwhile the Plains were becoming more and more flooded with whites, and conflicts between them and the Indians were increasing daily. For anyone who could read the signs, big trouble was ahead, and it could be expected that John Smith would be involved. But first he would enjoy an interesting interlude among the big cities of the East.

7

A Visit with Lincoln and Barnum

The Indian chiefs and squaws which are now exhibiting at the Museum, visited yesterday morning Public School No. 14, on Twenty-seventh-street, near Third Avenue. They were accompanied by Mr. Barnum and by Mr. Smith, who acts as interpreter. They were conveyed to the school in an omnibus drawn by six horses, which was preceeded by a vehicle containing a band of musicians. . . New York Times. [1]

The outbreak of the Civil War affected the course of John Smith's life just as it did all else in the nation, more so particularly because of the settlement of Colorado Territory just on the eve of hostilities and because the men who flooded the rivers and mountains in search of gold came from both northern and southern states. In the saloons and gambling houses and dirt streets of the mining towns, men argued, fought and sometimes dueled over the matter of secession, and a bitter struggle began between them over control of the Territory.

Southern men formed clandestine groups, practiced drilling, and sought to purchase all the firearms available. Northerners countered by buying all percussion caps to be found. One of the rebel leaders was balding, bearded Charley Harrison, who ran the Criterion saloon in Denver and had the reputation of being a dangerous gunfighter and killer. Another was fiery Park McClure, Denver's first

---

[1] *New York Times*, April 11, 1863.

postmaster who once held off the sheriff from the post office with a shotgun to prevent him from serving a warrant and whose temper resulted in a duel in which he was wounded in the groin.

But the Union forces under the leadership of newly appointed Governor John Evans quickly began to organize the Union men into the First Regiment of Colorado Volunteers with units stationed in Denver's new Camp Weld. When trouble began to develop in the area of the Criterion, Captain Sam Tappan aimed a cannon at the front door of the building and placed Harrison under arrest. Harrison was held in jail for a time, then put on a stage with a warning never to return to Denver. But others, including McClure, rode for Texas, only to be captured after raiding a wagon train at the Cimarron Crossing by troops from Fort Wise. They were returned to Denver, but soon escaped.

While the struggle for supremacy was going on in Colorado Territory, another crucial contest was being waged on the Plains for the affections of the tribes there. Texas had long had trouble with the Plains tribes, and before the Civil War began they had driven the Caddoes, Anadarkoes, Wichitas, Wacoes, Tawakonies, and Tonkawas from their reservations on the Clear Fork of Texas into the Indian Territory, now Oklahoma. On May 12, 1858, a party of Texas Rangers and some friendly Indians attacked a Comanche village on Little Robe Creek in the Territory, killing seventy-six warriors. A short time later, federal troops from Texas under Major Earl Van Dorn attacked a large band of Comanches who were on their way to peace talks, killing seventy more Indians. Still the powerful Kiowas and Comanches controlled most of the Northern Texas and Panhandle regions, and south to San Antonio and Mexico to plunder, kill, and take captives.

The Confederacy decided early in the war to enlist the

aid of the warlike tribes, and dispatched General Albert Pike, poet and early Western explorer, to make treaties with them. In August of 1861 he found a large encampment of Comanches and other tribes near the Antelope Hills in western Indian Territory and signed treaties with them. A copy of the Comanche treaty was brought into Fort Lyon by one of their chiefs, and Agent Boone immediately reported it to authorities, causing concern among Union officials.[2]

The Federal government had abandoned Indian Territory already, withdrawing their meagre forces from Fort Arbuckle, Fort Cobb, and Fort Washita into Kansas. A conference was held with the Osages, a strong and powerful tribe then assigned to a reserve in southeastern Kansas, asking them to report any strangers who crossed their lands. In May of 1863 they discovered a band of some twenty-three white men riding westward from Missouri across their reservation. A battle ensued, with the Osages pinning the men down on a sandbar of the Verdigris River where they finally killed and beheaded them all except two who managed to slip away and back to Missouri. In going through the effects of the dead men, it was discovered that all of them had been Confederate officers who were assigned the task of invading Colorado for the purpose of recruiting and stealing gold. Two of those beheaded were Col. Charley Harrison and Capt. Park McClure.[3]

It was also decided by the government to counteract the Confederate influence on the Indians in another manner. Major Samuel G. Colley,[4] cousin of Indian Commissioner William P. Dole, had been appointed to replace

[2] *Commissioner of Indian Affairs, 1861*, 714–15.

[3] "Massacre of Confederates by Osage Indians in 1863," W. L. Bartles, *Kansas Historical Society Collections*, VIII, 62–66. "The Only Survivor's Story of Massacre on Rebel Creek, 1863," *Independence Daily Reporter*, February 7, 1914.

[4] Harry Kelsey, "Background to Sand Creek," *Colorado Magazine*, vol. 45 (Fall 1968), 279–399.

Boone, whose loyalty to the Union was questioned by some, as agent for the Cheyenne and Arapaho tribes. Colley suggested that it might be a good idea to take a group of the Indian chiefs to Washington and impress them with the power of the Federal government. His cousin was in agreement.

Thus in January of 1863, John Smith was dispatched to go out, locate the Indians, and secure a delegation to visit the Great Father in Washington.[5] Smith found a large encampment, consisting of several tribes not far from Fort Larned at the mouth of Pawnee Fork. Not only were the Cheyennes and Arapahoes there, but also bands of Comanches, Kiowas, and Plains Apaches, plus some 300 Caddoes who had been driven out of the Indian Territory by the Texans, who had come in behind the retreating Union forces. All of the Indians were in a very destitute condition and suffering badly from disease and hunger, even though a Union officer had recently been among them vaccinating them for smallpox.

From these encampments, Smith gathered a number of chiefs: Lean Bear, War Bonnet, and Standing-in-the-Water of the Cheyennes; Spotted Wolf and Neva of the Arapahoes; Lone Wolf, Yellow Wolf, White Bull, Yellow Buffalo, and Little Heart of the Kiowas; Ten Bears and Pricked Forehead of the Comanches; Poor Bear of the Plains Apaches; and Jacob of the Caddoes. Two Kiowa squaws also went along.[6]

---

[5] *Commissioner of Indian Affairs, 1863*, 239–57.

[6] Left Hand of the Arapahoes was very upset that he was not chosen to go along. He claimed that Colley had left earlier than he had promised, while Left Hand was away, on the recommendation of Smith who did not like him. Smith did not want him to go to Washington, Left Hand claimed, because he could talk English and Smith would not be able to tell lies if he were along. Little Raven had refused to go without Left Hand. John J. Saville, Surgeon, 2nd Colorado Volunteers, to Mr. Holloway, Fort Lyon, Colorado Territory, April 15, 1863. Records of the Bureau of Indian Affairs, Cheyenne and Arapaho Indians, 1859–1939, Berthrong Collection, Oklahoma Division of Manuscripts, Norman, Oklahoma.

On March 12, 1863, these Indian chiefs accompanied by Major and Mrs. Colley and John Smith, arrived at Leavenworth, Kansas, where they were lodged overnight in the Planters Hotel. Here they were received as a frontier curiosity by Leavenworth citizens, and their photograph was made at the Addis Art Gallery.[7]

Lodging a wild Indian in a city presented certain complications, as Colley and Smith soon learned. Few of them had hardly even set foot inside a walled structure before, let alone eaten at a table or slept in a bed. Though Smith finally persuaded them to enter their hotel rooms, he found that they would have nothing at all to do with beds, preferring instead to spread their blankets on the floor. It was also necessary to furnish raw beef for them to "prepare in their own fashion."

The group left Leavenworth by a Majors' stage coach for St. Louis, the long, jolting ride offering another new experience to the horseback-adapted chiefs. At St. Louis the group changed to another unfamiliar mode of travel, the fire-spitting, smoking, clanging "iron horse" of the white man which had not as yet been seen on the Kansas plains. It was only with a great deal of persuasion that Smith managed to get them aboard, though once the wild Indians began to feel safe they thoroughly enjoyed themselves watching the countryside fly by outside the windows of the train. On March 26, the delegation arrived in Washington, D.C., home of the Great Father Abraham Lincoln.

The next morning the Indians, Major and Mrs. Colley and John Smith were escorted into the East Room of the White House for an interview with the President.[8] Because of the great novelty of the occasion, invitations had

---

[7] *Leavenworth Times*, March 13, 1863.

[8] *Washington Evening Star*, March 27, 1863. *Washington National Republican*, March 27, 1863. *Washington Daily National Intelligencer*, March 28, 1863.

been sent to the diplomatic corps, resulting in a large
assemblage of distinguished onlookers. These included
the secretaries of State, Treasury, Navy and Interior; the
Commissioner of Indian Affairs; the ministers of France,
Prussia, and Brazil and their families; lesser governmental
figures; and other notables such as the Washington social-
ite, Miss Kate Chase. Also present were members of the
press, their pencils flying across their notebooks with descriptions of the savages from the Plains.

The Indians, dressed in full regalia with buffalo robes,
bead-worked leggins, colorful feathers, and their faces
painted, were instructed by Smith to seat themselves in a
semicircle on the carpet at the far end of the room. They
were instantly surrounded by the curious crowd which
gaped and whispered at them. The chiefs were quite satisfied to be the center of so much attention.

It was a few minutes before the door opened, and President Lincoln entered. To the Indians, who had all their
life heard of the Great White Father in Washington, the
office had taken on myth-like proportions, and the tower-
ing, bearded Lincoln must have seemed god-like. One by
one, Smith called out the names of each chief. That chief
would then rise and give the President a vigorous shake of
the hand, then immediately resume his position on the
floor. Following Indian etiquette the young squaws were
not introduced.

When this formality was over, the President indicated
his willingness to hear the chiefs. Smith immediately announced that Lean Bear wished to speak, but the Cheyenne chief was so nervous that he would like to have a
chair to sit in while he talked. A comfortable arm chair
was quickly brought forward for him, and he seated himself.

"Tell him not to be at all backward," Lincoln instructed Smith, "but to say all he has to say with perfect freedom."

With Smith interpreting, Lean Bear spoke in the guttural Cheyenne tongue and sign language. He expressed his thanks to the Great Chief for his kindness and said that it was a pleasure for him to have this interview. The chiefs who had come with him were of different tribes, he said, but they were all glad to see the Great Chief of the white people and shake him by the hand and speak their hearts to him.

They had come a long way and wanted his advice and counsel on many matters concerning their situation. Lean Bear would hear all the Great Chief had to say, and when he went away he would not carry it in his pockets, but in his heart, out of which it could not be lost.

"The President," Lean Bear said, "is the great chief of the white people; Lean Bear is the great chief of the Indians. Our wigwams are not so fine as this; they are small and poor. Lean Bear hopes the great chief will look upon the Cheyenne with favor and say in his wisdom what would be best for them to do. The chiefs are here to listen to his advice and carry it in their hearts."

Lean Bear explained through Smith that many white people had begun to visit where he lived on the Plains. While he wished very much to keep peace with these people, he feared that there were many white men on the Plains who were not ready to keep peace with the Indians. He insisted that he would keep his people from starting trouble.

The Indians, he said, were sorry that there was great fighting between the white people themselves, but the Cheyenne did not want anything to do with it. They did not understand it and did not want to take sides with either the North or South. The Cheyennes wanted nothing but peace with the white man, and Lean Bear hoped it would last as long as he lived.

The Cheyenne chief ended his remarks by saying that he and the other chiefs were now a long way from home, their families were alone with no one to protect them, and he hoped the Great Chief would send them back as soon as he could. They were anxious to get home.

Lean Bear rose from his chair and took his seat on the floor once again. Smith then introduced another chief, who also expressed his hope for continued peace on the Plains.

"When I look around and see all these fine things," the chief said, "it seems like some kind of magic. I cannot tell how I got here, so far away from home. It seems that we must have come on wings, the same as a bird flies through the air."

When the chiefs had finished, President Lincoln indicated to Smith that he had a few remarks to make in return.

"You have all spoken of the strange sights you see here among your pale-faced brethren," Lincoln said, "the very great number of people that you see; the big wigwams; the difference between our people and your own. But you have seen but a very small part of the pale-faced people. You may wonder when I tell you that there are people here in this wigwam, now looking at you, who have come from other countries a great deal farther off than you have come.

"We pale-faced people think that this world is a great, round ball and we have people here of the pale-faced family who have come almost from the other side of it to represent their nations here and conduct their friendly intercourse with us, as you now come from your part of the round ball."

At this point Lincoln had an aide, a Professor Henry, bring forth a world globe, and the President laid his hand on it, saying that the professor would explain the "ball" and show where the Indians lived on it. Professor Henry then gave a detailed explanation of the formation of the earth with John Smith translating. The Indians were shown how much of the earth was water and how much was land, what countries traded with the United States and where Washington, D.C., was located on it in relation to their country.

We have people now present from all parts of the globe, [Lincoln continued,] here, and here, and here. There is a great difference between the pale-faced people and their red brethren, both as to numbers and the way in which they live. We know not whether your own situation is best for your race, but this is what has made the difference in our way of living.

The pale-faced people are numerous and prosperous because they cultivate the earth, produce bread, and depend upon the products of the earth rather than wild game for a subsistence.

This is the chief reason of the difference; but there is another. Although we are now engaged in a great war between one another, we are not, as a race, so much disposed to fight and kill one another as our red brethren.

You have asked for advice. I really am not capable of advising you whether, in the providence of the Great Spirit, who is the great Father of us all, it is for you to maintain the habits and customs of your race, or adopt a new mode of life.

I can say only that I can see no way in which your race is to become as numerous and prosperous as the white race except by living as they do, by the cultivation of the earth.

It is the object of this Government to be on terms of peace with all our red brethren. We constantly endeavor to be so. We make treaties with you, and will try to observe them; and if our children should sometimes behave badly, and violate these treaties, it is against our wish.

Lincoln then leaned forward toward Lean Bear and with a kindly smile on his face, observed, "You know it is not always possible for any father to have his children do precisely as he wishes them to do."

The President then shook hands with each of the Indians again and took his leave. When he had departed, the Indians were escorted to the conservatory to see displays of plant life. Here, at Smith's direction, the Indians were seated in a line on the floor and, with Mrs. Lincoln and the other women guests standing behind, their photograph was taken by an artist from Brady's studio.

The wish of Lean Bear and the others to return home quickly was not to be fulfilled. For several days after the interview, the Indian chiefs were entertained with tours of the capitol and even one evening at Grover's Theatre where they saw the romantic play "St. Mare."[9]

The time had almost come for them to return to the Plains when Agent Colley received an interesting letter from the famous P. T. Barnum in New York City. Barnum, always on the lookout for new marvels with which to fascinate the public, insisted that the chiefs be allowed to see New York and Philadelphia as well as Washington.[10]

"In my museum," Barnum wrote, "I can show them a million curiosities from all parts of the earth, and taking them to the top of the building, can present them a *coup d' oeil* of New York in its glory, wealth and maritime greatness, which will ineffaceably endure on their memories to the latest hour of their lives."

Barnum was really more interested in showing the Indians as a curiosity to New York, but he made an interesting offer, at least to Colley.

"I will recompense them with most valuable presents

9 *Washington Evening Star*, March 3, 1863.

10 *New York Tribune*, April 7, 1863.

SMITH AND MRS. LINCOLN

John Simpson Smith stands to the far left behind a group of Cheyenne and Arapaho Indians while Mrs. Abraham Lincoln is standing at
the far right. Next to Smith is Agent Samuel Colley.

Courtesy, Lloyd Ostendorf

while they stay here," he promised, "and will spare neither money nor pains in endeavoring to make them happy, and in securing the comforts of yourself and their interpreter."

Both Colley and Smith understood a good thing when they heard it, and the proposition was quickly accepted for the Indians. Smith, Commissioner Dole, Major Colley, and the Indian chiefs arrived in New York City on April 7 as guests of Barnum. The *Times* reported: "Barnum, it appears, has had to lay in for them an immense stock of raw beef, coffee, bread, red ochre, feathers and oil, they having never yet descended to the degradation of taking their dinner at a table d'hote, and using anything so absurd as a napkin . . . they will doubtless attract thousands to the museum."[11]

It was no coincidence that on the same day an advertisement appeared in the *New York Times* and other city papers:

> AN EXTRAORDINARY SIGHT IN NEW YORK. First Appearance of the GREAT INDIAN CHIEFS AND WARRIORS who have just arrived from Washington where they have been on a visit to their "Great Father," the PRESIDENT OF THE UNITED STATES all of them being fully attired in their WAR PAINT, WAMPUM AND FEATHERS and presenting the most attractive features of the REDMAN IN HIS NATIVE GRANDEUR fresh from the hunting grounds and WIGWAMS OF HIS WILD ABODES.[12]

The New York press reaction was mixed with wonderment and sophisticated ridicule of the "Untutored savages" who fought over the trinkets presented them and who basked in the attention of the gaping crowds. April 13, the *New York Times* commented:

> The Wild Indians still remain under the cheerful impression that they are the guests of the City, that Barnum is the Great Mogul, and the Museum is his palace. They are the genuine

---

[11] *New York Times*, April 8, 1863.　　　　[12] *Ibid.*, April 8, 1863.

animal, and make no mistake. Paint, feathers and trinkets cover their exterior; but their interior is, metaphorically speaking, filled with dead men's bones. They are a hard set, and, if Barnum is permitted to remain unscalped, he will do well.[13]

During this time, the chiefs continued to enjoy their part in Barnum's menagerie of comedians, "wonderful living hippopotamuses," melodrama stage plays, and other assorted wonders of the world. They were taken on tours occasionally, once to visit the Naval Yards, another time to visit a school where 1,500 children sang and did calisthenics for them.

Their appearance on Broadway and other streets through which they passed excited great attention, and by the time the building was reached, a large concourse of people began to assemble in the vicinity . . . The Indians appeared highly pleased at the calisthenic exercises performed by the children, and listened attentively to some delightful singing, although, of course, the words were unintelligible to them. "War Bonnet," upon being invited to speak, declined, for the reason that everything was new to him, and he could say nothing which would be satisfactory to those present. Before taking leave they stood in line, while Mr. Smith designated each one by his and her name, and the tribe to which they belonged, and also intimated their designations, giving "Yellow Buffalo" the credit of being the best Indian in the delegation, and "Little Heart" the discredit of being the worst one . . . The unique party remained about an hour, and were then conducted to the omnibus and driven down Broadway.[14]

Despite daily notices in the newspaper advertisements that each day was to be their last in New York, the Indians, with Colley and Smith, remained on and on. April 16 Barnum's ad announced that "Major Smith, the Interpreter of those Indian chiefs and warriors has unexpectedly been detained one day longer."[15] Then on the seven-

[13] *Ibid.*, April 13, 1863.

[14] *Ibid.*, April 11, 1863.

[15] *New York Tribune*, April 16, 1863.

teenth, the stay was extended again when the public was notified that Major Smith had agreed to stay two days more. Finally on April 18, the chiefs appeared on stage at Barnum's museum and made farewell speeches which Smith interpreted to the audience.

8

Abraham's Children

I want to say something. It makes me feel bad to be talking about these things, and opening old sores . . . Mr. Smith has known me since I was a child; has he ever known me to commit depredations on the whites?

Arapaho Chief Neva[1]

Though relations had been amiable between the chiefs and their hosts in the East, conditions on the Plains between the white and red man were to deteriorate badly that summer of 1863. Not surprisingly, John Smith was caught up in the thick of things.

In early July, with Fort Larned surrounded by a huge encampment of Indians, a guard at the post shot and killed a drunken Indian. Serious trouble almost developed before it was discovered that the Indian was a Cheyenne. Fortunately, not many Cheyennes were in the encampment. Still, the other more hostile tribes were fretful, and the threat of a general Indian war hung over the thinly garrisoned fort.

About the same time, Colorado Territorial Governor John Evans had heard in Denver that the Sioux, Cheyenne, and Arapaho tribes were uniting for a "war of extermination" against the whites on the frontier. As a result he dispatched Elbridge Gerry, who now operated a ranch in northern Colorado, to contact the tribes relative to

---

[1] Senate Executive Documents, 39th Congress, second session, No. 26. Hereafter cited as "Sand Creek Massacre."

holding a peace council. He also directed Agent Colley to send John Smith and his son Jack out from Fort Lyon for the same purpose.[2]

Gerry found 150 lodges of Cheyennes on the head of the Smoky Hill and held a council with their chiefs who agreed to meet Evans in September. The Arkansas River Cheyennes, however, told Smith that the trip was too far and their horses too poor and that they were busy making their lodges following a big buffalo kill.

The Smoky Hill Indians failed to show up to council with Evans in September when their villages were struck by whooping cough and diarrhea. Evans took this as a personal rebuff, and he was further dismayed when a Northern Arapaho, Roman Nose, met with him but refused to enter into any treaty agreement.

Toward the last of September Major Scott Anthony, new commander at Fort Lyon, made a tour from Lyon down the Arkansas to Larned, visiting camps of the Kiowas, Comanches, Caddoes, Plains Apaches, and Arapahoes with John Smith as his guide and interpreter.[3] The Indians, though destitute and suffering much from hunger and disease, all professed friendship and a desire for peace. But in November Colley sent Smith into the field again, and this time he reported back that he had located 160 lodges of Cheyennes and about 200 of Arapahoes. The Cheyennes were still angry over the killing of a brave at Fort Larned, believing it had been done by an

---

[2] *Commissioner of Indian Affairs, 1863,* 424. Upon his return to the Plains, Smith on June 27, 1863, wrote a letter to Commissioner of Indian Affairs W. P. Dole asking about a salary increase to $800 or $1,000 from $400 per annum which he felt had been promised by Dole and Charles E. Mix while in the East. He said that since his return from Washington both he and the agent had been very busy among the Indians endeavoring to keep them quiet. (Smith to Dole June 27, 1863, Letter copy from National Archives)

[3] *War of the Rebellion, Official Records of the Union and Confederate Armies,* series I, vol. XXII, part II, 571–72. Hereafter cited as *Rebellion Records.*

INDIAN CHIEFS ARRIVE IN DENVER

The Cheyenne and Arapaho chiefs (second wagon) arrive in Denver in September 1864, to meet with Governor Evans. John Smith is in the first wagon with the released captive white children and his son, Jack.

Courtesy, State Historical Society of Colorado

Osage in the service of the government. Smith also reported that there was a tough band of Sioux on the Arkansas and another on the Smoky Hill offering the war pipe to tribes in those areas. He feared the Indians might go to war.[4]

Smith could read all the signs. The country was changing, much too fast. For one thing, there was the basic distrust which the second generation of whites on the frontier held for the Indians. And almost as suspect to them were the old frontiersmen, squawmen like Jim Beckwourth in Denver, Charlie Autobees and his half-breed sons who ranched along the Arkansas, and "Uncle John" Smith at Fort Lyon.

Politics, too, had begun to wax heavy in Colorado. Governor Evans had teamed up with Colonel John M. Chivington, the ex-Denver preacher who had won military recognition in the Colorado First's defeat of the Texas Confederate Army at La Glorieta Pass. Together they seized upon the Indian situation as the issue of the day. Evans walked the streets of Denver with a sixgun strapped to his side, while Chivington, now commander of the Military District of Colorado, demanded not only that the Colorado First troops be kept at home to protect the white settlers but that the Colorado Second Regiment be withdrawn from its Civil War assignment and returned to Colorado Territory.

Mother Nature also contributed to the tension among the whites on the Colorado frontier. In May of 1864 an unpredicted and calamitous flood roared down Cherry Creek from the mountains, washing away a good part of Denver, most of which had been precariously constructed in the creek bed. That summer a grasshopper plague swept across the grassy plains east of the mountains, de-

---

[4] *Commissioner of Indian Affairs, 1863*, 542–43.

vouring crops. A feeling of calamity was in the air, and with the memory of the Minnesota Sioux uprising of 1862 still fresh in people's minds, Denver citizens watched the Indian situation nervously.

That fear was laid bare following the massacre of Ward Hungate and his wife and two children southeast of Denver on July 11 by a party of Northern Arapahoes. Governor Evans and Colonel Chivington seized upon the affair to insist to Union officials that Colorado would be in dire peril if any Colorado First units were withdrawn for Civil War duty.

A few days after the Hungate affair, Denver went into sheer panic when a false alarm of Indian attack was sounded, driving people to places of refuge. The alarm had been sounded by a frightened rancher who saw shadows moving in the dark while out looking for his cattle.

Evans requested and was granted authority to call up a regiment of mounted one hundred-day volunteers on grounds that the Indians were about to launch a "war of extermination" against the whites in Colorado. Thus, the stage was set for the fateful year of 1864, which was to see the problem of the Indians of the Central Plains come to a crisis and explode into the Indian War of 1864. John Smith was destined to play a key role in it all.

Trouble began in the spring of 1864 when two cases of cattle theft, supposedly by Indians, were reported to Denver authorities. As a result, Chivington began ordering Colorado First troops into the field with instructions to "Be sure you have the right ones, and then kill them." Several clashes between white troops and Indian bands in northern Colorado followed. On April 12, Lieutenant Clark Dunn and fifteen mounted troops fought a brief engagement near Fremont's Orchard on the South Platte with a band of Cheyennes who were driving some loose stock. On April 26, Major Jacob Downing, having received a report that Cheyennes had stolen horses from a South Platte ranch, found a village of eleven lodges which he attacked and destroyed. Early in May, Downing struck another Indian camp near Cedar Bluffs.

Meanwhile, operating out of Denver, Lieutenant George S. Eayre campaigned along Beaver Creek in eastern Colorado, locating two deserted Cheyenne villages which he burned. Then on May 1, Eayre commandeered fifteen light wagons off the streets of Denver and headed eastward along the Republican River, crossing military district lines into Kansas, with the intent of killing any Indians he encountered. On May 16, Eayre's command came across a large buffalo hunt three miles from the Smoky Hill River north of Larned. Heading the hunt was Cheyenne chief Lean Bear.

Upon seeing the approaching column of troops, Lean Bear rode out to meet them, carrying a paper which had been given to him in Washington, testifying that he was a friendly Indian and could be trusted. He also wore a peace medal on his chest. With him was another Indian named Star. When the Cheyennes were within a short distance of the troops, the soldiers commenced firing, killing both Lean Bear and Star.[5] As President Lincoln had said, it was not always possible for a father, even the Great Chief, to get his children to behave as he wished.

It was this unnecessary and unwarranted killing of Lean Bear that drove an enraged Cheyenne Nation to a bloody war against the whites during the summer of 1864, striking furiously against Kansas wagon trails and frontier settlements, murdering, plundering, scalping, and revengefully, taking white prisoners. Colorado, from

[5] *Rebellion Records*, series I, vol. XXXIV, part IV, 402–04. "The Chivington Massacre," 75.

whence the initial blow was struck by Chivington, was virtually untouched by the Cheyenne vengeance.

In June, Governor Evans issued a proclamation to "the friendly Indians of the Plains," directing them to come into various forts for protection.[6] On Evans' request, John Smith rode northward and delivered it to the tribes. Smith had continued to serve as official interpreter for Major Colley at Fort Lyon as well as for the military post which now had a new commander in Smith's old friend from Denver days, Major Edward W. Wynkoop. In July, Chivington himself arrived on the Arkansas for an inspection trip from Pueblo to Fort Larned. His guide was John Smith, whom he found "to be at home night and day" on the whole route. During this trip a band of Indians approached the stage coach in which Chivington and Smith rode but were driven off after an exchange of gunfire. It later proved to be Jack Smith with some Indian friends, riding out to greet John.[7]

Wynkoop arrived at Fort Lyon with strong intentions of carrying out Chivington's policy of killing every Indian he came across without asking questions. During the summer, however, his attitude toward the Indians changed markedly despite increasing difficulty along the Arkansas. Undoubtedly, John Smith was a prime influence on Wynkoop's Indian posture. This influence was especially obvious in September when three Indians were captured near Fort Lyon and placed in the guard house.

Smith was called in to help Wynkoop interrogate the prisoners—who were identified as a Cheyenne sub-chief named One-Eye, whose daughter was married to a rancher named Prowers and lived across the river from the fort; One-Eye's Cheyenne wife; and a buck named

---

[6] *Rebellion Records*, series I, vol. XLI, part I, 963–64.

[7] *Ibid.*, part II, 660.

Min-im-mie.[8] They brought with them a letter from Cheyenne principal chief Black Kettle, suggesting that the Indians wished to talk peace. They wanted someone to come out and hold a council on it.

At first Wynkoop was skeptical, fearing that this might well be a trap. But John Smith convinced him that One-Eye was sincere and that he could trust the word of the Cheyennes if he should go out and talk with them. On September 6, with Smith serving as a guide and scout, Wynkoop led a force of 127 mounted troops out of Fort Lyon, accompanied by the Cheyenne hostages: After a four day march, Wynkoop met with the main body of the Southern Cheyenne and Arapaho tribes on a branch of the Smoky Hill in western Kansas. On the following day, Wynkoop and his officers talked with the main chiefs of the two tribes. John Smith was assisted in interpreting for the council by George Bent, who was with the Indian encampment.

Through Smith, Wynkoop was successful in persuading the chiefs not only to give up their white prisoners as a token toward peace but also to come with him to Denver where they could counsel with Governor Evans. Black Kettle arranged for the release of four white children held captive by the Indians, then led his own band of Cheyennes into Fort Lyon. These acts were, in part, testimony to the trust and respect which the Cheyennes held for "Blackfoot" Smith.

At Lyon the chiefs were loaded into wagons, along with Smith, and escorted to Denver. The wagons, sprouting two American flags and escorted by a company of cavalry, arrived in Denver on September 28. There they were

----

[8] Detailed accounts of this and the ensuing expedition into the Indian country can be found in "Sand Creek Massacre." Also Edward W. Wynkoop's Unfinished Manuscript (Colorado History MSS II-20, Colorado State Historical Society).

MAJOR WYNKOOP AT FORT LYON

Major Edward W. Wynkoop, commanding at Fort Lyon prior to the
Sand Creek Massacre, relied upon Smith's services as a guide and
interpreter for many years.

greeted by a procession of buggies from the city and a photographer who recorded the event for history.

Wynkoop, who had ridden ahead of the chiefs, was chagrined to discover that Governor Evans was highly resentful of his peace-making efforts as Superintendent of Indian Affairs for Colorado Territory. The governor finally gave in and conceded to meet with the Indians at Camp Weld in Denver. Colonel Chivington was there, along with several prominent Denver citizens, the seven chiefs, and Wynkoop's party. Smith, of course, did the interpreting during the meeting.[9]

For someone who feared an all-out war against the whites in Colorado, Evans was certainly unconciliatory in talking to the chiefs. He began the council by quizzing the Indians on recent troubles and accusing them of starting the fight at Fremont's Orchard. The chiefs answered his question without hesitation, but when it became apparent that the meeting was leading to more bitterness than toward a search for peace, Arapaho chief Neva spoke: "I went to Washington last year, receiving good counsel; I hold on to it. I am determined always to keep peace with the whites. Now, when I shake hands with them they seem to pull away. I came here to seek peace, and nothing else.[10]

The meeting concluded when Chivington took the floor to have his say:

> I am not a big war chief, but all the soldiers in this country are at my command. My rule of fighting white men or Indians is, to fight them until they lay down their arms and submit to military authority. You are nearer Major Wynkoop than any one else, and you can go to him when you are ready to do that.[11]

---

[9] "Sand Creek Massacre," 213–17, contains Report on Camp Weld Meeting. Present at the meeting were Cheyenne principal chief Black Kettle, Chief White Antelope, Dog Soldier leader Bull Bear, and Arapaho chiefs Neva, Bosse, Heaps of Buffalo, and No-ta-nee.   [10] *Ibid.*, 216.   [11] *Ibid.*, 217.

When Smith had made the interpretation for them, Black Kettle and the other chiefs rose and shook hands with all the whites around the room, satisfied and pleased that the first major war between the Cheyennes and the whites had come to an end, or so they thought.

When the meeting was over, the chiefs were arranged before a camera and their photograph taken.[12] Standing behind them dressed in a coat, vest, and high collar with a bow tie and looking more like a Denver merchant than a man who had lived for more than thirty years in the wilderness, was John Smith. At his side, looking far more white than Indian, was his son Jack.

Wynkoop and Smith escorted the Indian chiefs back to Fort Lyon, there holding another council. Wynkoop then instructed them to go out and bring in their families and villages, promising them full protection of the fort. Within ten days, Arapaho chiefs Left Hand and Little Raven brought some 113 lodges of their tribe in, 652 Indians. But on November 4, Major Scott Anthony arrived at Fort Lyon with orders from District Headquarters at Fort Riley, Kansas, to relieve Wynkoop as post commander, placing an entirely new perspective on the whole matter.

Though Anthony was saying otherwise in his official reports, he declared to Wynkoop, with whom he had fought side by side at La Glorieta, that he would continue the other's Indian policies. When Black Kettle arrived with sixty of his men, having left his village at the big

---

[12] This much-published but classic picture of the chiefs at Denver is one of the few known photographs of John Smith, third from left in back row, and the only known photograph of Jack Smith, second from left in back row. Dexter Colley stands second from right in back row. The Indian chiefs are often misidentified. Certainly Black Kettle is the man seated in the center holding the peace pipe. Seated to the far left is probably White Antelope, since he bears striking resemblance to the White Antelope whose picture was taken in 1851 while visiting Washington. The Indian to the right of Black Kettle fits Wynkoop's description of the "hulking" Bull Bear.

bend of Sand Creek about forty miles north of the fort, Anthony called a council with Smith and John Prowers interpreting.[13] The Indians were told they should hold their village at Sand Creek because there were no rations to issue them.

Black Kettle was satisfied with this reassurance, especially since it was given to him by Wynkoop and Smith, and took his party on upriver to visit William Bent at his ranch. The Indians returned the next morning and were given food by Prowers. Anthony, who had promised to ride down and talk with them again, instead sent Smith to reassure them once again that they would be perfectly safe at Sand Creek.[14] Black Kettle and his party left, joined by the Arapaho Left Hand who was ill, while Little Raven moved his Arapahoes down the Arkansas to the mouth of Sand Creek.

On November 26, Wynkoop departed Fort Lyon by stage for Fort Riley. On that same morning Anthony called in John Smith, who also had been ill, and asked him to ride out to the Sand Creek village and ascertain the number of Indians there.[15] Smith was willing, for Dexter Colley had a load of trade goods which he wanted taken to the village.[16] Also, his squaw and Jack were with Black Kettle's band and he wished to see them.

[13] "Sand Creek Massacre," 46, 87, 104–06.
[14] "Massacre of Cheyenne Indians," 17–18.   [15] "Sand Creek Massacre," 128.
[16] Private Louderback states that Major Anthony asked Smith to "go out there and see what the Indians were doing, and gave him permission to take some goods out with him to trade. . . ." Ibid., 134.

Smith was subjected to charges that he was partner to Dexter Colley in trading the Indians their own annuity goods, some claiming the two men were getting rich from it. John Smith certainly never accumulated any wealth at any time in his life, and no real proof exists that he was involved in a conspiracy with Colley. Smith testified: "Mr. D.D. Colley had some provisions and goods in the village at the time, and Mr. Louderback and Mr. Watson were employed by him to trade there. I was to interpret for them, direct them, and see they were cared for in the village. They traded for one hundred and four buffalo robes, one fine mule, and two horses." "Massacre of Cheyenne Indians," 11.

DENVER COUNCIL, SEPTEMBER 1864

In this famous, but often mis-identified photo, John Simpson Smith stands third from left; his son, Jack, second from left. Squatting in front are Major E. W. Wynkoop and Captain Silas Soule. Cheyenne principal chief Black Kettle is directly behind Wynkoop, while the Dog Soldier chief, Bull Bear, is seated second from right. The Indian seated at the far left is White Antelope.

Courtesy, State Historical Society of Colorado

He was accompanied by Watson Clark, a teamster in the employ of Colley, and a private from the fort named David Louderback. It took the three of them a day and a half to make the trip, arriving in the Indian camp shortly before noon on the twenty-seventh, finding a hundred or more lodges camped in a nook of the creek where a small range of mesquite-spotted sand bluffs bent its southerly flow. Smith and the two men unloaded the trade goods into the lodge of Chief War Bonnet, unhitched their mules to graze and fed themselves. That afternoon and all the next day, the three traded the goods for buffalo robes, horses, and mules.[17]

For Smith, it was almost like the old days as he relaxed in the lazy comfort of the Indian village, conducting the trade and enjoying the day-time warmth of a clear, windless sky. He had no way of knowing as he crawled into his blankets that night that on the morrow the colorful era of Indian trade on the Arkansas River would be forever ended, that even at that moment Colonel Chivington was marching toward the Sand Creek village with a small army.

[17] "Sand Creek Massacre," 128, 135.

9

Murder at Sand Creek

When the troops first approached I endeavored to join them, and was repeatedly fired upon; also the soldier who was with me, and the citizen. When the troops began approaching in a hostile manner, I saw Black Kettle, head chief, hoist the American flag over his lodge, as well as a white flag, fearing that there might be some mistake as to who they were. . .
John Smith.[1]

During the summer of 1864, Indian trouble broke with new fury over the plains of Kansas and Colorado. War parties of Cheyennes and Arapahoes, their horses' tails tied up for battle and paint streaking their angry countenances, fell upon the isolated ranches and settlements from the Arkansas to the Platte. Near Fort Lyon three men were killed, and a party of Arapahoes under Raven's Son raided Charlie Autobees' ranch south of the river, driving off his horse herd. On August 21, two men were killed and scalped just west of Lyon.

Major General S. R. Curtis, commanding the Department of Kansas, decided upon a punitive expedition against the Cheyennes and Arapahoes, and in September he took to the field with a command, moving south out of Kearny. Curtis' forces hunted their way to the Solomon River, finding plenty of buffalo but no Indians. He was in camp on the Solomon when word arrived that a Confed-

---

[1] "Sand Creek Massacre," 128.

erate army under General Sterling "Pap" Price had crossed the Arkansas toward Kansas. The news brought his Indian hunt to an abrupt end.

In Colorado Territory, the Third Regiment of one hundred-day volunteers was becoming the joke of Denver funsters who had dubbed them the "Bloodless Third." Outposts at Fort Lupton, Valley Station, and other places had failed to yield any satisfactory action. With it becoming apparent that the Indians had been driven from the South Platte, temporarily at least, Chivington began moving units of the Colorado First and Third to Bijou Basin, southeast of Denver.

Late in October, Brigadier General P. E. Connor arrived from Salt Lake City, announcing that he intended to go Indian hunting in Colorado. Chivington was considerably upset by Connor's presence, and he immediately issued orders moving the Colorado Third, plus three companies of the Colorado First, toward the Arkansas River. The weather was bitterly cold, with several feet of snow on the ground, when Chivington joined his forces at Camp Fillmore on the Arkansas on November 18.

The Colorado force now marched westward along the north bank of the river for Fort Lyon, arriving there on the twenty-seventh and being warmly received by Major Anthony. Chivington immediately threw a cordon of pickets around the post, allowing no one to leave under penalty of death. Robert Bent, William's oldest son, who lived near Fort Lyon, was pressed into service as a guide, supplementing the ailing Jim Beckwourth, who had been brought from Denver by Chivington.

When the Fort Lyon officers learned of Chivington's intention to attack the Cheyenne's Sand Creek camp, several of them protested strongly. Most vocal was Captain Silas Soule, a fiery ex-Kansas Jayhawker who had once

attempted to rescue John Brown from his cell at Harper's
Ferry. Chivington threatened to place Soule in irons. Major Anthony, however, willingly added his Fort Lyon
troops to those of Chivington's small army, and at 8 p.m.
on the twenty-eighth of November, the force of about
seven hundred men began their nighttime march towards
Sand Creek, forty miles to the north.

It was a crispy cold but clear night, and the command
moved in columns of four, all mounted, with four mule-
drawn mountain howitzers and the supply wagons bump-
ing along behind. Some of the men nibbled on hardtack,
some warmed themselves with liquor, others tightened
their coats against the chilled night air. Some of them had
talked pretty big about killing Indians and the scalps they
were going to take, but now just about everybody felt
some apprehension about the fight ahead of them. The
silence of the land which now seemed to swallow up their
small talk was a reminder that these untamed rolling hills
of eastern Colorado were still the domain of the Indian.

November 29, 1864, broke brisk and clear. John Smith,
who had shared a lodge with his two helpers and his son
Jack, rose early and was eating breakfast when a squaw
poked her head inside the lodge flap and jabbered in
Cheyenne that there was a big cloud of dust to the south,
indicating that a "heap of buffalo" was coming. This
struck Smith as being peculiar for this time of year, but
he went on with his meal. As he was finishing, a Cheyenne
chief came into the lodge and said that a big force of
soldiers was headed toward the camp. He wanted Smith
to go out and find out who they were and what they
wanted.[2]

Someone suggested they might be Fort Lyon troops,
but Smith shook his head, having just talked with Anthony

---

[2] *Ibid.*, 135.

three days before. Private Louderback agreed; there had
been no plans for any movement by Fort Lyon troops.
They reasoned, therefore, that if soldiers were coming
then it must be General Blunt's men from Fort Riley.
Smith felt disposed to make certain Blunt was informed as
to the recent developments with the Indians.

Hurrying outside the lodge, Smith and the others saw
that blue-coated horsemen were crossing the river southeast of the camp, and the popping sound of pistol fire
reached their ears. Jack Smith headed toward the horse
herd east of the camp, but the troops were already cutting
between the herd and the village. Quickly Smith and Private Louderback found a lodge pole and tied a white
handkerchief to the end. Holding it high, Smith advanced
towards the troops, reasoning that dressed as he was in a
soldier's overcoat, a hat, and trousers, it was unlikely that
he would be taken for an Indian. No matter whose troops
these were, they surely would not fire on another white
man.

As he advanced, another body of troops poured over
the edge of the sand bluffs and began taking up positions
along the opposite side of the creek. Suddenly bullets
began to whiz past Smith, close enough that there was
little doubt that he was their target. About that time he
heard someone across the stream yell, "Shoot the old son
of a bitch, he's no better than an Indian!"[3]

John Smith knew well enough the resentment many
whites on the frontier held for squawmen, and he knew it
was time for him to get out of there. He stood frozen for a
moment, not daring to make an abrupt move. It was at
that moment that Private George Pierce, a member of the
Colorado First Regiment who had distinguished himself

---

[3] *Ibid.*, 138.

at La Glorieta in a similar act of bravery, galloped his horse forward from his lines in an attempt to rescue Smith. Pierce never made it to the frontiersman; he was killed before he reached him. But Pierce and his horse did block the line of fire at Smith long enough for him to escape back to the lodge, no doubt saving the life of the Cheyenne interpreter.[4]

The teamster Clark now tied a tanned buffalo hide on a lodge pole and stood on the wagon, waving it at the attackers until he was forced by a fusillade of bullets to get down. The men retired to the questionable safety of the lodge, watching the battle develop and trying to determine what the fight was all about.

From the lodge opening, Louderback spotted the hulking form of Colonel Chivington as he rode across the creek at the lower end of the village. Louderback stepped from the lodge and hailed him. Chivington recognized the soldier and told him to come on and he would be safe. But even as he advanced, Louderback was fired upon until Chivington ordered it stopped.

John Smith, too, yelled at Chivington and was recognized. The officer told "Uncle John" to bring his friends and fall in with the command.[5] Thankfully, Smith left the lodge and attached himself to one of the Fort Lyon mule-drawn caissons and moved with it upstream, half-running and half-riding. Around him the Cheyenne village had exploded into panic and chaos. The Cheyenne men, mostly old chiefs and elders, attempted in vain to halt the avalanche that had fallen upon them.

White Antelope walked with hands raised towards the troops in hopes of talking with them, but he served only to make a good target for the eager soldiers who riddled his

---

[4] *Ibid.*, 49, 65.   [5] "Massacre of Cheyenne Indians," 6.

body with bullets as he stood in the middle of Sand
Creek.[6] Women and children, following the custom of all
Plains tribes, attempted to make good their escape on the
side away from the attack. Some of them followed the
snaking bed of Sand Creek northward, some hiding in the
cut banks of the creek and many taking refuge in a
swampy cattail hole where the troops quickly discovered
them. Smith, testifying before a Congressional investiga-
tion, later described this part of the massacre of the people in the hole:

> By the time I got up with the battery to the place where these
> Indians were surrounded there had been some considerable fir-
> ing. Four or five soldiers had been killed, some with arrows and
> some with bullets. The soldiers continued firing on these Indi-
> ans, who numbered about a hundred, until they had almost
> completely destroyed them. I think I saw altogether some sev-
> enty dead bodies lying there; the greater portion women and
> children. There may have been thirty warriors, old and young;
> the rest were women and small children of different ages and
> sizes.
>
> The troops at that time were very much scattered. There
> were not over two hundred troops in the main fight, engaged in
> killing this body of Indians under the bank. The balance of the
> troops were scattered in different directions, running after small
> parties of Indians who were trying to make their escape.[7]

When the action had quieted down, Smith was advised
to stay in the lodge where Zerepta and young William
Gilpin had remained throughout the fight. The soldiers
were still out for blood, and many of them had been
drinking. No half-breed or even any white man who had
been associated with the Indians was safe.

Chivington's force, Smith learned, was comprised of
units of the Colorado First, including the Fort Lyon command, and of one hundred-day volunteers who formed the

---

[6] "Sand Creek Massacre," 73.   [7] "Massacre of Cheyenne Indians," 6.

COLONEL JOHN CHIVINGTON
Chivington led the infamous attack by Colorado troops against Black
Kettle's village at Sand Creek.
Courtesy, Denver Public Library Western History Collection

Colorado Third Regiment. The Third had been raised that fall from Denver and other settlements by Evans and Chivington especially to protect Colorado against the Indians' supposed war of extermination. Many of the men saw themselves as avengers for the death of the Hungate family which had been killed and scalped by Northern Arapahoes near Denver in June.

The Cheyenne wife of Charlie Windsor, the Fort Lyon sutler, was brought to the lodge which held Smith, and shortly afterwards Jack Smith who had escaped during the attack but later gave himself up, was brought in. Later in the evening three young Indian children and a month-old papoose which had been found on the battlefield were brought in.

The fighting had simmered down by the middle of the afternoon, and soldiers and officers alike began to scour the Cheyenne camp for souvenirs, which included scalps taken from dead Indians. Later in the evening, John Smith was called from the lodge by an officer and asked to help identify the Indian dead. He accompanied the man over the field of battle, making identifications of the ones he recognized, some with whom he had been friends for many years. Besides White Antelope, whose body had been mutilated by soldiers, Smith found the remains of One-Eye; Standing-in-the-Water and War Bonnet, both of whom had been to Washington with Lean Bear; No-ta-ne, one of the chiefs who visited Denver; famous old chief Yellow Wolf; and many others. One badly cut-up body he mistook for Black Kettle, who had somehow managed to escape.[8]

Smith remained in the lodge with his family that night. Once, when some soldiers appeared and confiscated all of

[8] "Sand Creek Massacre," 128.

their robes and blankets, Smith went to Chivington and complained. As a result, guards were placed on the tent, but at noon of the next day the soldiers left and did not return.

The liquor in camp had done nothing to improve the already murderous mood of the troops, and Jack Smith, who eighteen years before had been such a delight to Garrard, became a matter of much concern to some of the soldiers. Though well known to the Fort Lyon soldiers, having worked on haying crews at the post, Jack was a prime target for the hatred of the boisterous "Bloodless Third" troops. No matter that he was the son of "Uncle John" Smith; the important thing was that he was half-Indian and had been living with the Indians in their camp. Much loud talk about killing Jack circulated around, and the men were restrained only by the fact that Chivington might not like for them to kill one of his prisoners. But then, others argued, hadn't Chivington ordered them not to take prisoners in the first place?

Lieutenant Dunn, who had been involved in the Fremont's Orchard clash with the Cheyennes in April, felt Chivington out on the matter of killing Jack. Chivington, not wanting to be held responsible, answered that Dunn need not ask since it was already known how he felt. Major Anthony later testified:

> I went to Colonel Chivington and told him that Jack Smith was a man he might make very useful to him; that he could be made a good guide or scout for us; "but," said I to him, "unless you give your men to understand that you want the man saved, he is going to be killed. He will be killed before tomorrow morning, unless you give your men to understand that you don't want him killed." Colonel Chivington replied, "I have given my instructions; have told my men not to take any prisoners."[9]

9 "Massacre of Cheyenne Indians," 22.

Another officer testified: "I heard him (Chivington) say we must not allow John Smith and family, father of Jack Smith, to be harmed; that he did not intend to take any Indians prisoner."[10] Clearly, to the troops, Jack Smith was Indian enough. On the afternoon of the day following the battle, ten to fifteen men, including some of Dunn's troops, came to the lodge where Jack Smith was being held. Private Louderback described in testimony what happened:

> In the afternoon there were several men in talking to Jack Smith, and told him that he was a son of a bitch, and ought to have been shot long ago. Jack told the man that was talking to him that he did not give a damn; that if he wanted to kill him, shoot him. When Jack said this I thought it was time for me to get out of there, as men had threatened to hang and shoot me as well as uncle John Smith and the teamster that was with us.[11]

Old Jim Beckwourth (Beckwith), the mulatto mountainman who had won fame with Fitzpatrick and Jedediah Smith as a trailblazer of the early West and who had been taken as a guide by Chivington upon leaving Denver, was also in the lodge when the soldiers returned later and witnessed the murder of Jack Smith:

> He (Jack Smith) was sitting in the lodge with me; not more than five or six feet from me, just across the lodge. There were ten to fifteen soldiers came into the lodge at the time, and there was some person came on the outside and called to his father, John Smith. He, the old man, went out, and there was a pistol fired when the old man got out of the lodge. There was piece of the lodge cut out when the old man went out. There was a pistol fired through this opening and the bullet entered below his (Jack Smith's) right breast. He sprung forward and fell dead, and the lodge scattered, soldiers, squaws, and everything else. I went out myself; as I went out I met a man with a pistol in his hand. He made this remark to me; he said, "I'm afraid the damn son of a

---

[10] "Sand Creek Massacre," 177.   [11] *Ibid.*, 136.

bitch is not dead, and I will finish him." Says I, "Let him go to rest; he is dead." . . We took him out and laid him out of doors. I do not know what they did with him afterwards.[12]

John Smith, meanwhile, had been called away by a soldier who walked him towards Chivington's tent, some sixty yards away. When they were within a few feet of the Colonel, who was standing by his campfire, Smith heard a gun fired and saw a crowd run towards the lodge. Then someone came over and told Smith that Jack had been killed.

Officers in sympathy with Chivington attempted to cover up the murder. Major Anthony wrote his brother that, "We, of course, took no prisoners, except John Smith's son, and he was taken suddenly ill in the night, and died before morning."[13] Major Sayr, Colorado Third officer, wrote in his diary that Jack Smith was killed accidently while looking at a gun, but he goes on to admit that "some of the boys dragged the body out onto the prairie and hauled it about for a considerable time."[14] Chivington, of course, said nothing at all about the sordid business in his official reports.

The murder of Jack Smith was virtually forgotten in the controversy which arose over the massacre of the Indians. The feeling of most whites in Colorado was expressed by the *Rocky Mountain News* when it congratulated Chivington on his victory over the "Thieving and marauding bands of savages who roamed over this country last summer and fall . . . "[15] The one hundred-day volunteers of the Third paraded down Denver's streets as

[12] *Ibid.*, 71.

[13] "The Chivington Massacre," 92.

[14] Hal Sayre, "Early Central City Theatrical and Other Reminiscences," *The Colorado Magazine*, vol. VI (1929), 47–53.

[15] *Rocky Mountain News*, Denver, December 30, 1864.

heroes, some of them even displaying their bloody tro-
phies of war on the city stages.

But outcries, principally from Wynkoop and other Colorado First officers who supported him, soon reached
Washington, D.C. Wynkoop was ordered back in command of Fort Lyon as the Army prepared to conduct a
military hearing of the Sand Creek affair. On January 15
at Fort Lyon, John Smith gave his affadavit account of the
events beginning with One-Eye's appearance at Lyon
through Chivington's massacre of Black Kettle's village.
This was used both by the Army hearings conducted in
Denver under Lt. Colonel Samuel Tappan and by a Joint
Special Committee of the two Houses of Congress under
Congressman J. R. Doolittle.

In March of 1865 Smith accompanied a group of Colo-
radoans to Washington, D.C., to give testimony before the
Committee on the Conduct of the War, B. F. Wade,
Chairman. Also testifying were Colonel Jesse Leavenworth, Captain S. M. Robbins, Dexter Colley, Major Scott
Anthony, Agent Samuel G. Colley, Governor John Evans,
and A. C. Hunt, U.S. marshal for the District of Colorado.
Smith again repeated the story of Sand Creek as he experienced it.

After hearing from the seven men, the committee cen-
sured both Evans and Anthony severely and concluded
concerning Chivington: ". . . the truth is that he surprised and murdered, in cold blood, the unsuspecting
men, women, and children on Sand creek, who had every
reason to believe that they were under the protection of
the United States authorities, and then returned to Denver and boasted of the brave deeds he and the men under
his command had performed."[16]

---

[16] "Massacre of Cheyenne Indians," 2.

10

War in Kansas

On one occasion I was with Captain John Smith, a guide and interpreter. There was an Indian brilliantly arrayed making signals. Captain Smith pulled out a small mirror from his bosom and flashed it on the Indian, who became frightened and ran away. . .   General Winfield Scott Hancock.[1]

The massacre of Black Kettle's band of Cheyennes marked the end of a way of life on the Central Plains and the beginning of a new era of conflict. Sand Creek signaled a clear-cut call to hostilities by the Indians, providing strong evidence for the war elements of the tribes even in far-off camps of the Sioux, Comanches, Kiowas, and others who were already suspicious about the intentions of the white men. In truth, Sand Creek was the initial strike in a war between the Indians and the whites for supremacy on the Plains.

Eastern Colorado was virtually eliminated as a part of the Cheyenne-Arapaho range, just as the South Platte was no longer available to them for winter camps. Now the tribes were secure only in the rough, ravine-slashed land of western Kansas, where small game was difficult to find even for the best hunters and where the great buffalo herds had been reduced by the promiscuous slaughter by whites over the past thirty years. Even there the Indians

---

[1] *New York Tribune*, Sept. 2, 1867.

had no assurance that another blue-coated column would not come charging down upon their camp.

So now along the Smoky Hill, the Solomon, the Republican, and other rivers of western Kansas, the Cheyennes and Arapahoes and visiting war parties of Sioux danced and sang their anger into the night sky and made vengeful harangues against the pale-skins who had stolen their lands, diminished their game, and murdered their people. No longer could the old chiefs hope to restrain the young bloods whose entire culture was based upon warriorhood, who had been taught from birth that death in battle while protecting his people was a high honor, and whose very manhood was synonymous with his courage in battle and his ability to kill his enemies.

The massacre at Sand Creek also marked another important change in the situation on the frontier. A second generation of whites had now taken command. Men like William Bent, Kit Carson, and John Smith were no longer listened to for advice on Indian matters. Though the government would call upon them once more in an effort to leash the dogs of war loosed by Chivington, these men were now looked upon by frontier whites as "squawmen" and "Indian lovers" who were more allied to the Indian cause than to that of the whites and who were not to be trusted. The mountain man, with his wild, rough ways and his free, untamed spirit, and his fanciful tales of the old days, was no longer the Western hero. His day had ended with finality at Sand Creek.

The new generation of whites had not known the Indian tribes when they were an independent and proud people, before they had been made degenerate by the white man's whiskey and driven to near-starvation by lack of game. These white men had not lived among them, received the hospitality of their lodges, or learned to know them as people. Instead, they saw the red man as a heathen who begged and stole along the wagon roads; as a murdering savage who killed, raped, scalped, and took white women and children captive and made slaves of them; as a barbarian who stood in the way of national growth and civilization.

Sharing much the same views were the frontier military. Following Sand Creek, which occurred just a few months before the end of the Civil War, the Federal government began moving troops westward, and ambitious military men were prone to the same attitudes as the white settlers that "the only good Indian is a dead Indian," and that the only way to solve the Indian problem was to kill them off like the buffalo.

For John Smith, Chivington's massacre of the Cheyennes marked the end to the Indian trade as well as pointing with finality to the fact that the time of unlimited freedom in the American West was at an end. But of greatest importance to him was that he stood between two cultures, that of the red man and the white man, with allegiances to both but suspected and distrusted by the Indian war societies on one side and the frontier military on the other. Though he would still be able to maintain his friendships with the old chiefs and with the peaceably-inclined Indian Bureau, his position in the period of conflict following Sand Creek was an uncomfortable and dangerous one.

Chivington's massacre of Black Kettle's village stirred up a controversy among the residents of Colorado Territory which quickly spread to Washington and throughout the nation. *Rocky Mountain News* editor Byers and many other prominent citizens of Colorado were quick to

champion the act as justified and necessary, arguing that
the Indians were known to be guilty of crimes of murder
and thievery, that it was altogether clear that the Indians
were hostile from the fortifications and the white scalps
which Chivington's men reportedly found in Black Kettle's camp.[2]

Others, however, saw the attack as a wanton attempt
to gain prestige for Chivington and Evans and as a violation of an officially-made promise of safety and refuge.
Chief Justice Benjamin Hall protested to Washington officials, as did Colonel Tappan, who was a newspaper correspondent for some eastern papers. Major Wynkoop was
infuriated and made an official demand for an investiga-
tion. The War Department responded by quickly setting
up a board of inquiry which convened February 1, 1865,
in Denver.

The first witness was Captain Soule, who had refused to
order his men to fire on the Indians at Sand Creek and
who now defied threats against his life to testify. He was
joined by other Colorado First officers who served under
Wynkoop.

Chivington, however, had already resigned his commis-
sion, his term in service having expired even before the
Sand Creek attack. Soule, appointed provost marshal of
Denver, was murdered on a Denver street one night soon
after being married, and another Fort Lyon officer, Lieu-
tenant Cannon, was poisoned to death in the Tremont
House shortly after bringing in Soule's killer from New
Mexico.

John Smith now found himself more of a man-in-the-
middle than ever, suspected by Indians and whites alike of
being an ally of the enemy. "The implacable enmity of

---

[2] *Rocky Mountain News*, Denver, December 29, 1864, 2.

the Cheyennes against the whites had cut him off from all communication with this nation."[3] Still, in the inevitable search for peace, Smith's interpreting talents and Indian experience would ultimately play an important role in the difficult years ahead.

Smith spent the spring and summer of 1865 at Fort Lyon, where Major Wynkoop had been restored to command. These were hectic and hostile days on the Plains, with the Cheyenne Dog Soldiers striking out from their camps in western Kansas, joined by the angry Sioux and northern bands of Cheyennes and Arapahoes, an estimated 2,000-plus warriors.

Early in February, 1865, while the Army hearing was going on in Denver to determine the guilt of Chivington, more than a thousand warriors struck Julesburg on the South Platte in northern Colorado, burning buildings and taking a considerable amount of provisions. They also raided along the Platte road, killing travelers, burning wagons, taking whatever goods and stock they could find. Victory dances and war drums sounded long into the night along the Republican, and warriors talked of a "war to the knife" against the white man.

Not all the Indians had taken to the war path, however. Black Kettle, with "shame as big as the earth"[4] at leading his people into such a death trap, had gone south of the Arkansas with about eighty lodges, there joining with Little Raven's band of Arapahoes. But with small parties of hostiles striking along the Arkansas River road as well as along the Platte and Smoky Hill, it was virtually impossible to tell which bands were committing depredations.

A punitive expedition against the Indians was planned

---

[3] *New York Herald*, December 12, 1868, 8.

[4] *Commissioner of Indian Affairs, 1865*, 704.

by Major General Grenville Dodge in an effort to protect the frontier, but these efforts were halted when President Johnson authorized Senator Doolittle's Congressional committee to make new treaties with the Plains tribes. The committee toured the Arkansas Road and visited Fort Lyon in June where they talked with John Smith and others about the Indian situation.[5] Traveling on to New Mexico, Doolittle met with Kit Carson and William Bent, who felt that they could make a lasting peace with the Indians if given the opportunity. The Senator was convinced, and a treaty council was arranged for at the mouth of the Little Arkansas River, near present Wichita, Kansas, in the fall of 1865.

Once again John Smith was sent out to help gather in what he could of the Southern bands, and when the treaty council was held in mid-October, he was employed as the official interpreter for the Cheyennes, making it the third occasion on which he stood between the tribe and the government in helping to make an important treaty. Through Smith, Black Kettle told the commissioners:

> I once thought that I was the only man that persevered to be the friend of the white man, but since they have come and cleaned out (robbed) our lodges, horses, and everything else, it is hard for me to believe white men any more . . . As soon as you arrived you started runners after us and the Arapahoes, with words that I took hold of immediately on hearing them.[6]

With Smith's help the commissioners convinced these Southern bands to accept a new reserve south of the Arkansas River and to work towards reestablishment of peace between their people and the whites. Thirty-one mixed bloods among the Cheyennes and Arapahoes were each granted a section of land from the 1861 reservation

---

[5] "The Chivington Massacre," pp. 49–52.
[6] *Commissioner of Indian Affairs, 1865,* 704.

in Colorado, and among them were two of John Smith's children, William Gilpin, who was now in school at Council Grove, and a daughter named Armana.[7]

Despite the treaty, the fact remained that the Indians were badly split and the Dog Soldiers on the Republican were just as hostile as ever. In an effort to reunite the Cheyennes, Wynkoop was assigned to the chore as a special agent of the Interior Department.[8] He immediately hired John Smith as his scout and interpreter. In February of 1866, with bitter cold gripping the Kansas plains, Wynkoop and Indian Agent I. C. Taylor delivered several wagon loads of trade goods under escort by cavalry units from Fort Dodge to Black Kettle's Cheyenne village forty miles southeast of Dodge. John Smith was already in camp there with his family, acting as a sort of watchdog for Wynkoop.[9]

Wynkoop talked with the Cheyenne Dog Soldier leaders, Medicine Arrows and Big Head, and secured their promises not to raid against the whites in the future. Two incidents of note also occurred during this visit. In one of them a trader named Boggs cheated some Cheyennes by trading the unwitting bucks eleven one-dollar bills for eleven ten-dollar bills. When the Indians found out they had been taken, they came back looking for Boggs, who had by then reached the safety of Fort Dodge. But the Indians came across Boggs' young son on the road away from the fort and killed him in revenge.

The other matter was much happier. While at the Cheyenne camp, Smith, who was also trading for the firm of Morris and Hanger, learned of a sixteen-year-old white

---

[7] C. J. Kappler, ed., *Indian Affairs, Laws and Treaties.* vol. II, (Washington: GPO, 1904), 889.

[8] Berthrong, *The Southern Cheyennes*, 264.

[9] Records of War Department, Fort Dodge, Letters Sent, March 5, 1866.

girl, Mary Fletcher, who had been captured on the North Platte and was being held prisoner by Sand Hill's band of Cheyennes. Smith entered into negotiations with the Indians and purchased her freedom, turning the girl over to the military escort.[10]

Although the Dog Soldiers had remained relatively quiet during the spring and early summer of 1866, Smith, William Bent, and Ed Guerrier were in constant touch with the bands. They warned authorities that the Indians would not surrender their hunting grounds on the Smoky Hill, which the government wanted for the construction of the Kansas-Pacific railroad.[11] Smith, who spent most of the summer of 1866 with the Cheyennes, was with Wynkoop on August 11 when he met with eight Cheyenne chiefs on the Smoky Hill and discussed their moving south to the new reservation area.[12] In September, I. C. Taylor reported that he had left "Captain John Smith, U.S. Interpreter," with the Indians who were then holding their fall buffalo hunt on the Smoky Hill. Smith was to remain with them and report any hostile demonstrations.[13]

Though the Dog Soldiers created no major disturbances during that summer, in late August Roman Nose and Spotted Horse began visiting stage stations along the Smoky Hill and threatening the employees if they did not leave the country in fifteen days. On September 19 a party of Cheyennes stampeded the Fort Wallace horse herd.

In order to secure approval of Senate amendments to the Treaty of the Little Arkansas, two special agents were

[10] *Ibid.*, Hyde, *Life of George Bent*, 251.

[11] Berthrong, *The Southern Cheyennes*, 260.

[12] Wynkoop to Colley, August 11, 14, 1866, Upper Arkansas Letters Received.

[13] I.C. Taylor, Fort Zarah, Sept. 30, 1866. *Commissioner of Indian Affairs, 1866*, 280.

assigned by the Bureau of Indian Affairs to talk with the Cheyennes and Arapahoes at Fort Zarah during October with John Smith interpreting. William Bent was contracted to haul a large amount of annuity goods to that post for disbursement. But things did not go well. The Dog Soldiers, more recalcitrant than ever after securing a supply of liquor, threatened the peace-inclined chiefs such as Black Kettle and Little Robe to withdraw their support of the amendments, one of which removed the Cheyennes and Arapahoes from Kansas entirely and limited them to Indian Territory.[14]

At the same time, a party of forty Cheyennes under Bull Bear attacked a stage station on the Smoky Hill and killed two men. This, and the murder of one of Bent's men by Medicine Arrow's son, interrupted the council, but after much coaxing by Wynkoop and Smith and the distribution of presents, the talks were resumed. The difficulties faced by the peace-inclined chiefs were indicated by Black Kettle's speech:

> Black Kettle—The questions you have asked us regarding the killing of two men at Chalk Bluffs and running off stock from Fort Wallace I knew nothing about, having never heard of it before. The Sioux have been in stealing our horses and have stolen horses around this place and have probably killed the man and stolen the stock you spoke of. Mr. Smith your Interpreter was with us nearly all last summer—(Mr. Smith stated that he had never heard of these depredations before, except some fleeting rumors around here) and he knows we are not guilty. I have heard from some of the last Indians that came in, that the Sioux had taken seven horses from the Smoky Hill and that the Dog-soldiers had taken them from them and were bringing them in. The Sioux have stolen horses from the Cheyenne and the Dog

14 Wynkoop to Commissioner Bogy, November 26, 1866; Wynkoop to Murphy, December 2, 1866, Upper Arkansas Agency, Letters Received; Hancock to Davidson October 21, 29, 1866; Hancock to Carleton, Hancock to Ben Holiday, October 23, 1866, Department of the Missouri, Letters Sent.

soldiers have recovered them. White Horse, a Cheyenne, went with a party of men and took seven horses from the Sioux and returned them to the whites, four more horses are still in the possession of the Sioux belonging to the whites. Ever since we made peace at the Little Arkansas my heart has been with my word, I have suffered much and been for peace. Ever since we crossed here in the summer to go North, Smith has been with us and has been trying to get us to come back. At Fort Ellsworth you promised us to be back in six weeks, we came here and waited until we were tired and then went south—I told Col. Bent and Mr. Smith that I was mad and not to send for me.

Notwithstanding the promises made to me had not been fulfilled, when we heard that Commissioners were here and had sent for us, chiefs and soldiers got on their horses and came to hear what you had to say. It is very hard for us to move so often, and we are without proper clothing, yet we have come again to see you as you requested—We do not approve of the killing of the white man (Mexican) by one of our foolish young men. We have come here to arrange it in some way. What is right is all we want. The reason why we moved from this place so soon as we did was to get away from trouble, by remaining here we were liable to get into trouble, if all had left when I did, the murder would not have occured. Ever since we made peace last fall at mouth (of) Little Arkansas river we have been promised that when our goods came out, wherever we were or wherever we were directed to go there we were to receive our goods. We did not leave here angry or object to receiving our goods, but left through necessity hoping that you would have these goods issued to us in our villages according to your promises. The distance is too far for us to come in for our goods. I have never refused to obey your calls and have always come when sent for, but it is hard for us to obey your request to come back with our villages to receive our goods at this time. You are here again as a Chief sent here to represent the Great Chief at Washington. Your talk is all good and we are going to listen to you. Will it be true, or as heretofore not come out as you represent it. We will leave once again, there may be some jumping around yet, but we will trust you.

Our women and children at this season are not in condition to come here, and if you can take our goods where we can camp we would be highly pleased.[15]

When Little Bear and Roman Nose, who was there as a warrior and not as a chief, were asked to sign the treaty amendments, they both stubbornly refused. Roman Nose rose before the council and made a short speech which expressed the view of the Cheyenne warrior:

> Roman Nose—I have made peace with the troops in the North (meaning at Fort Laramie). I did not come here for a coat or something to eat. I came here to listen to what you had to say about the killing of the white man (Mexican). If I talked all day the whites would pay no attention to it. I do not believe the whites. I do not love them. If I had plenty of warriors I would drive them out of this country. But we are weak. The whites are strong. We cannot count them. We must listen to what they say. At the treaty made at the North the Commissioners did not speak of making roads on the Smoky Hill. Our nation is not properly represented here. Therefore we should not speak for them.
>
> Captain Bogy—I wish all your tribe to be represented in Council when we talk about the murder.
>
> Roman Nose—Goods and provisions . . . Troops are brought here to drive us from it. We made peace with the whites on the North fork of the Platte. We have kept it. Every time we meet with whites in Council we have new men to talk to us. They have new roads to open. We do not like it. I did not come here to represent myself as a chief but as a soldier.[16]

After the council, Wynkoop moved his agency closer to the Indian country at Fort Larned. Meanwhile, Major General Winfield Scott Hancock, then commanding the Department of the Missouri, decided to conduct a campaign against the Indians who had committed the Smoky Hill depredations and began moving troops towards

---

[15] Report of a council held at Fort Zarah, Kansas, November 10, 1866, with the Arapahoe and Cheyenne Indians of the Upper Arkansas Agency.

[16] Ibid.

Larned, arriving there on April 9, 1867, with his command. Wynkoop was instructed to warn the Indians that
Hancock was prepared for war if they did not stop their
raiding, and he sent Smith and Ed Guerrier out to request
that the chiefs come in for talks.[17] They did so, riding
their thin horses through deep snow to Fort Larned where
Hancock held a council with them, Smith and Guerrier
interpreting.[18]

During the talks Hancock told them that he intended to
march his force to their village, which was reported to be
some thirty-five miles up the Pawnee Fork from Larned.
The chiefs, remembering Sand Creek, were greatly
alarmed at the idea of having their village threatened by
troops again. Smith reported this to Wynkoop, who protested against the march to Hancock. But the General was
adamant and on the next day ordered his troops into their
saddles.

He encamped several miles from the village, and again
sent word to the chiefs that he wished to talk with them.
When the chiefs did not arrive at the time designated,
Hancock broke camp and advanced. Within six miles he
met the Cheyennes, about three hundred of them. Hancock immediately deployed his troops in a long cavalry
line with sabers drawn. It was a classic confrontation of
white and Indian armies.

Two reporters for Eastern publications were present at
the Hancock meeting with the Indians: Theodore Davis
of *Harper's New Monthly Magazine*, and Henry M. Stanley, a young, roving reporter who was destined to gain
fame in Africa as the discoverer of Livingstone and as an

---

[17] Letters Sent, Department of the Missouri, May 7, 1867, Captain Mitchell to
Col. E. Wynkoop, Camp near Fort Harker.

[18] Little Robe later told George Bent that even the interpreters—Smith, Dick
Curtis and Ed Guerrier—could not even make out what Hancock meant. Hyde, *Life of
George Bent*, 257.

WYNKOOP AND HIS INTERPRETER, JOHN SMITH
This sketch by T. R. Davis appeared in the May 11, 1867, issue of
Harper's Weekly. Copied by Oklahoma Univ. Division of Mss.

explorer. Among the many curiosities which they found upon the plains of Kansas was a frontier notable named John Simpson Smith. Davis' description of an incident involving Smith is strong evidence that the old breed of frontiersman was no longer in vogue, having been replaced by younger, more dashing men such as George Armstrong Custer who were building their reputations as Indian fighters.

> Some of the Scouts, Guides, Interpreters, and Couriers-Adjuncts (sic.) headquarters for the first weeks of the campaign, if in liquor—a history and a mystery at best. To one of them who took pains to verify by statement each and every narrative, Custer one day said "John Smith, (he claimed this name) you should return from whence you came. Unquestionably your fort is Lyon." Possibly the man was 60 years old—but I doubt it, although after listening one day to some what disconnected and voluminous story of his performances—in which he was encouraged by Stanley and myself who in turn interrupted him with questions—we figured him out to be on his own mention of years spent in various localities—137 years old. Our promptness in spreading this information made John Smith so sad and mad, that he left camp after nightfall, and we saw him no more—Generals Hancock and Custer commenting on the circumstances concluded that a prolonged stay of John Smith at Fort Lyon whither we believed he had gone, might occasion a change in the orthography of the name of that post.[19]

Davis had a similar reaction to Wild Bill Hickok: "Wild Bill sauntered up. Seeing he was not welcome, the Scouts stay was short and starting off remarked with some irony, 'Ther's another dodgasted sardine of a newspaper cuss (Stanley) bunken in the sutler's shack what wants my wind, I see you don't.' "[20]

Hancock, however, continued to make much use of

---

[19] Theodore R. Davis, "Henry M. Stanley's Indian Campaign in 1867," *The Westerner's Brand Book 1945–46*, x (Chicago), 104.

[20] *Ibid.*

Smith's talents as a guide, scout, and interpreter. In May following the confrontation with Roman Nose, the General dispatched Smith once more to bring in the Cheyenne chiefs and principal men for talks prior to marching to Fort Harker where he joined Custer and turned the Indian campaign over to the young officer.[21]

Hancock had done little more than stir up the Indians who had been relatively quiet during 1866. The Cheyennes responded to his visit during the summer of 1867 by striking the Kansas-Pacific railroad track-laying camps. Custer tried without success to chastise the Indians, and the Kansas plains again blazed into open warfare. John Smith continued to act as Wynkoop's contact with the peaceful bands, Custer obviously preferring to use others for his scouts.

Meanwhile, Congress had established another peace commission, and plans were laid to hold another big council with the tribes, hopefully to establish a permanent peace with them and to win clear title to the lands of western Kansas. And, once again, John Smith would be cast in a vitally important role in the affair which would come to be known as the Treaty of Medicine Lodge.

---

[21] Letters Sent, Department of the Missouri, May 7, 1867. Captain Mitchell to Col. E. Wynkoop, Camp Near Fort Harker.

11

The Medicine Lodge Council

Early in the morning, long before day-break Col. Murphy and John Smith, the interpreter, together with the Indian chiefs went ahead to prepare the way for us, for we agreed to be at Medicine Lodge Creek on the 13th, and now we can not reach it til the 14th, tomorrow. Today we rolled over the prairies for about five miles, when the scouts came across a piece of white card that fluttered in the breeze, being tied to a stake, and set right in the middle of the road. Around it was twenty four buffalo chips. The card had written on it: ''Be on your guard. Keep to left, eastwardly. John Smith.'' . . .

George Center Brown.[1]

In July of 1867, Congress established an Indian Peace Commission for the purpose of settling the Indian problem on the Central Plains for good, wishing especially to remove the tribes from the area of western Kansas where they were impeding the transportation, communication, and expansion of the railroads. It was hoped that the commission could separate the friendly Indians from the hostile and place them on reservations in Indian Territory.

The seven-man commission met in St. Louis in August and made preliminary plans for the feeding and treating of the Indians, while the various bands of Cheyennes, Arapahoes, Comanches, Kiowas, and Plains Apaches were being contacted and talked in. From there, the commis-

---

[1] *Cincinnati Commercial*, October 21, 1867.

sion moved to Fort Leavenworth where they heard testimony of frontier-experienced men concerning the Indian problem in Kansas. They then embarked up the Missouri River to Omaha and on to Fort Laramie where they councilled unsuccessfully with the Northern tribes.

In early October the commission reassembled at Leavenworth and took a train via Lawrence to Fort Harker. Here they joined the entourage of infantry, artillery, and Seventh Cavalry troops under Major Joel Elliott which would escort their caravan of wagons and ambulances to Fort Larned and on to the council site at Medicine Lodge Creek in southern Kansas. Accompanying the commission was a group of newspaper reporters who had been assigned the chore of covering the treaty council for many of the major newspapers of the nation.

While the commission was en route, John Smith had been busy helping Indian Superintendent Thomas Murphy and Major Wynkoop in contacting and convincing the various bands to come in to the council. Together with George Bent, who had been living in Black Kettle's village, Smith found the Cheyennes encamped on both the Cimarron and North Canadian rivers. Black Kettle, Smith learned, had been threatened by the Dog Soldiers against participation in the treaty talks. Nevertheless, Smith persuaded Black Kettle to come to Fort Larned along with the Arapahoes where they met with Murphy and Wynkoop on September 8.[2]

Indian-hating citizens of Kansas were much against treating with the Indians and highly skeptical of those associated with them. The October 3, 1867, issue of the *Leavenworth Conservative* spoke out bitterly against John Smith:

---

[2] Berthrong, *The Southern Cheyennes*, 292.

What makes matters worse is, when a treaty has been concluded there is always misunderstanding among Indians as to terms. That is in great measure due to misstatements made by interpreters. What dependence can be placed on a man who has resided among Indians for forty-five years, has two or three squaws, and children by the score educated to Indian habits? Such are facts in connection with John Smith, chief Interpreter at Big Medicine Lodge.[3]

Through Smith, Murphy directed the chiefs to take their tribes to Medicine Lodge Creek, some sixty miles south of Larned.[4] There Murphy, Wynkoop, and Smith joined them in late September with provisions for feeding their people. Ed Guerrier was sent to the Cheyenne camps on the Cimarron River with an invitation to the hostiles under Bull Bear, Tall Bear, Roman Nose, Medicine Arrows, and Big Head.

In early October, Wynkoop and Smith were back at Larned, when on October 11 Wynkoop received the commissioners and entertained them and reporters in the back room of the sutler's store where they had a chance to meet and drink with the redoubtable Kiowa war chief, Satanta.[5] Among other things, the commissioners were impressed as to how much of Satanta's paint came off on them every time he gave them an Indian hug. The commission left Larned on the day following for Medicine Lodge Creek.

With the Arapahoes and the main force of Cheyennes still out but the other tribes impatient to begin, the council got underway on October 19:

As per set time, we are met in a large, beautiful cottonwood grove, whose hallowed grandeur is rich. Stately trees lift high

---

[3] *Leavenworth Conservative*, October 3, 1867.

[4] Berthrong, *The Southern Cheyennes*, 292–93.

[5] *Chicago Times*, Oct. 22, 1867; *Cincinnati Commercial*, October 21, 1867.

their silvery tops, whose fullness the autumnal frosts have not yet affected. Here on the north bank of Medicine Creek, in a circle space of two acres, where the underbrush has been cut out, around which are dense brush thickets, beneath a leafy shady bower made by laying green bushes across long, green poles, resting in forks, driven in the ground, we are sitting. The Commission are sitting in a half circle facing the Indians who are sitting in full circles around us. The interpreters, John Smith, for the Cheyennes; J. H. McCloskin (McCusker) for the Comanches and Kiowas; Mrs. Virginia Adams, a half breed Indian, for the Arapahoes and Apaches, are standing in the open circle, where also are the correspondents. The council will soon move off. A breeze is creeping softly through the leafy branches of the tree. A genial smile of joy rests upon the countenances of the Commissioners and the Indians alike. General Harney, sitting in the center, to the left of Commissioner Taylor, had his full uniform in rig. Generals Augur and Terry are at the right of Mr. Taylor; both are in full military dress. Senator J. B. Henderson and Col. Sam F. Tappan are on the left wing. Along and beyond the outer circle are hundreds of Indian ponies, and Indian mules, and Indian horses, with U.S. stamped on the left shoulders. In the circle are hundreds of red men, women and children sitting in circle groups.[6]

The commissioners councilled with the Indians for two days, during which time many speeches were made by both the whites and the Indian chiefs. Senator Henderson read his address which he had written out, and it was translated to the tribes by Smith, McCusker, and Mrs. Thomas Fitzpatrick Adams, an Arapaho half-blood who was the widow of Thomas Fitzpatrick.[7] Bespeckled Ten Bears and Silver Broach talked for the Comanches, Satanta and Satank for the Kiowas, Poor Bear for the Apaches, and Little Raven for the Arapahoes, Grey Head for the Cheyennes, but only to say that he would wait until the other Cheyennes arrived. Black Kettle maintained his silence also during these talks.

---

[6] *Cincinnati Gazette*, October 26, 1867.

[7] *Chicago Times*, October 29, 1867.

MEDICINE LODGE COUNCIL

Though not identifiable in this sketch of the 1867 council, John Smith played an important role as chief interpreter for the Cheyenne and Arapaho Indians.

Copied by Oklahoma University Division of Manuscripts

On the 21st of October the Kiowas, Comanches, and Apaches signed the treaty document drawn up by the commissioners. The main body of Cheyennes still had not shown up, but that evening after dark, as a hard rain struck the camp, John Smith appeared at one of the commissioners' tent with several Cheyenne chiefs. Black Kettle was along, but also were several others who had not been present before, including Little Robe and White Horse from the hostile camps on the Cimarron.[8]

Smith told the commissioners that the Cimarron chiefs had just arrived and wished a short conference with Black Kettle before talking with them. With the wind pounding against the tent, the chiefs huddled with Black Kettle, who appeared to be considerably upset by the conversation. When they had finished, the chiefs then turned to Commissioner Taylor and said that they had finally decided that they would come in to the council, but insisted that the Kiowas and Comanches stay at the council as they wished those tribes to hear what they had to say.

Taylor finally agreed, and the chiefs said they would bring in their bands when they had finished with their medicine arrow ceremonies. Smith asked them when this would be, and Black Kettle explained through him that it would take about four days. This placed the commissioners in argument among themselves, with Senator Henderson much against the delay as well as allowing the Kiowas and Comanches to stay in camp. Finally Commissioner Taylor, speaking for the group, asked Smith to tell the chiefs that the delay was acceptable and the Indians would be expected in four days. That done and goodbyes said, Smith led the Indians out into the stormy night to their ponies.

---

[8] Douglas C. Jones, *The Treaty of Medicine Lodge* (Norman: University of Oklahoma Press, 1966), 137–38.

It was five days, on October 27, a Sunday, before the Cheyennes made it to council. During that time a great deal of fear had developed around the camps among both the whites and the other Indian camps, even the Arapahoes, that the much-feared Dog Soldiers of the Cheyennes were going to attack unexpectedly. The long wait, coupled with fears which were expressed by Little Raven of the Arapahoes, left the camp unnerved. Tension was increased even more when Bull Bear, leader of the Dog Soldiers, came in for a visit one day and said that he feared those Cheyennes under Roman Nose, who had recently threatened to kill Wynkoop because of Hancock's burning of the Cheyenne village, would not come.

Henderson and others of the commission were all for signing up the peaceful Cheyennes without waiting for the hostiles, but Wynkoop and Comanche Agent Colonel Leavenworth both warned that if they did, the Cheyennes might well be angry enough to attack the camp after the friendly Indians had gone.

> This awakened a feeling in the breasts of the Commissioners which did not console them much in their sleep, and "something was wrong, they knew, all the time. They were not going to remain here any longer at the peril of their lives." But Captain John Smith, who had lived with the Cheyenne thirty years, poured the oil of gladness on their heads by telling them that a young Cheyenne who had just come in had told him that their medicine council was over, and that now they would be in, certainly, on the 27th (Sabbath next). He (the young buck) had been sent in to tell them.[9]

When the Cheyennes did come, they came with style "like an army with banners."[10] The first evidence of them was a huge dust cloud which appeared over the distant hills on a quiet Sunday morning. Everyone in the camp,

[9] *Cincinnati Gazette*, November 4, 1867.
[10] *Chicago Tribune*, November 4, 1867; *Cincinnati Commercial*, November 4, 1867.

including the Indians, was seized with alarm, not knowing what to expect. Then as the camp watched with a sense of panic, the far ridges to the south of camp suddenly sprouted spearheads and gun-barrels. The sun glistened off the silver gee-gaws that decorated the Cheyenne horses as they swept en masse over the ridge and fell out of sight into the valley. For what seemed a very long time, they were gone, and the camp could hear only the occasional sounds of bugle notes drifting across the prairie, the echoing of a rifle shot, or Cheyenne "hi-ya, hi-hi-ya's."

The Arapahoes clustered fearfully together, while the Kiowas and Comanches quickly mounted and drew themselves up in fighting groups. The commissioners and reporters stood anxiously in front of their tents, intrigued by this view of impending Plains Indian hostility yet fearful for their lives. John Smith hurried over to the commissioners and reassured them that their fears were unfounded, that the Cheyennes were coming in peace. He was the only person in camp who felt very sure about it.

The noise of the Cheyenne advance grew louder, though the camp could catch only occasional glimpses of them through the trees. Finally they broke into view across the bed of Medicine Lodge Creek, five columns of some 400–500 Cheyenne warriors. The braves and their horses were decked out in full Cheyenne regalia. Some of them wore crimson blankets, some blue soldiers' coats which had either been issued to them at some council or had been taken from a victim in a raid. Many wore eagle-feather headdresses, beautifully ornamented with silver and brass, while their feet were decked with red and blue bead-worked moccasins. Above their heads they brandished a variety of weapons, including rifles, pistols, tomahawks, lances, and bows and arrows. It was a scene not soon to be forgotten by the white men who were feeling the alarms of pending danger in their bellies.

It was much to the commissioners' credit that they stood their ground as the Cheyennes sounded a bugle and charged across the creek bed in five separate columns and came to a dusty halt about fifty yards from the camp, there forming a vibrant line of prancing horses and war-chanting warriors. The commission, in full dress itself, was led to meet the Cheyennes by John Smith and George and Charlie Bent. The Cheyenne sing-song chant suddenly stopped, and several chiefs advanced to meet the white men.

This would be the last great show of Cheyenne prowess, their final chance to display before the world of the white man the might and splendor of their tribe which less than a century before had been at the mercy of the northern tribes. Historically, it was the final moment of glory for the Cheyenne Nation which had once ruled the Central Plains.

Smith made the introductions all around, the chiefs and the commissioners giving one another big hugs of friendship, and then helped to escort the chiefs to the tents where tobacco and coffee were provided. Having had reports of some Kaw Indians in the area, the Cheyennes did not wish to risk loss of their horses with so many of their warriors gone from their camp, so they did not remain to talk that day. But on the morning following, fourteen of their chiefs returned and sat down for a counsel with the commission.[11]

Henderson again served as spokesman for the commission, with Smith interpreting, telling the Cheyennes that a treaty had been prepared for them similar to the one

---

[11] *Cincinnati Commercial*, Nov. 4, 1867; *Missouri Democrat*, Nov. 2, 1867.

signed by the Comanches and Kiowas. When the Cheyennes were offered the floor, Little Robe passed the honor
of speaking first to Little Raven of the Arapahoes. Raven
recognized General Harney and "Mister Smith" as having
been at the Little Arkansas council. He requested that the
Arapahoes be provided a reservation in Colorado, which
he said he considered to be his rightful home.

The first Cheyenne to talk was Buffalo Chief, who laid
claim to all the land between the Platte and Arkansas as
defined by the 1851 treaty. This touched upon the sorest
point of all, since the prime purpose of the treaty for the
whites was to remove the Indians from that region. The
commission went into a discussion of the problem among
themselves. Senator Henderson, extremely anxious to
have the treaty completed and be gone, insisted that he
could get the Cheyennes to sign, and he called John Smith
and George Bent to one side and talked with them.[12] None
of the reporters were included, so they could report that
after a while some of the Cheyenne chiefs were asked to
join them. They saw the group hold a brief discussion and
one of the Indians, Buffalo Chief, reach out and take Henderson by the hand as he spoke to him. Smith and Bent
then talked emphatically to the chiefs who seemed to
respond favorably to the words and then return content-
edly to their groups.

Henderson later told the reporters what had been said.
He had requested that Smith tell the Indians that they
need not enter their reservation areas right away and
could continue to hunt between the Platte and Arkansas
so long as the buffalo remained, though the Indians were
not to go nearer than ten miles to any white settlement.
When the buffalo were all gone, the Indians would take

---

[12] *New York Herald*, Nov. 1, 1867; *New York Tribune*, Nov. 6, 1867.

up their permanent homes in Indian Territory. Accepting this, the Cheyenne chiefs agreed to sign the treaty document.

But the matter was not completely resolved. When the signing time came, all of the Cheyennes put their mark on the paper except Bull Bear, White Horse, and Little Robe. When Smith asked why he was not signing, Bull Bear said that there were already enough marks on the paper. Smith talked with the three chiefs and finally convinced them that in order to please the White Father they should sign, as one reporter put it, "Before the polls were closed."[13] Reporter Stanley, still disdainful of Smith as Davis had been, gave a different but interesting account of the signing:

> The treaty lay drawn up in full, with all the requisite technicalities in it. The Cheyennes were impatient for their goods. Some idiot had commenced to break open the goods ready for distribution. The Cheyenne were bound to go and watch the interesting proceedings. The Commissioners were in a sweat. What was to be done? Smith, the interpreter, stood hard by—a self-willed, obstinate old fellow. "I say, Smith, those Cheyennes have not signed the treaty yet; bring them up to sign," said some one, and away went the old gentleman, the long coat tails flapping behind with the excitement which burned within him . . . It took half an hour to convince Bull Bear that he was in duty bound to sign. At last Gen. Harney got up, and brought up an argument in this wise: "The Great Father knows you are a chief, and your name must be seen upon its face, or he will not recognize it." This was a socdolger, he signed it at once and, instead of touching the pen lightly, he pressed on the head of the pen until it was buried in the paper. He then turned for all, with a grim smile, and said, "I have done it, and my word shall last. One Chief is enough to sign for us, but here are a dozen names."[14]

[13] *Missouri Republican*, November 2, 1867.

[14] *New York Tribune*, November 8, 1867.

Another Stanley account said:

> The interpreter, Smith, was dispatched in pursuit to urge the
> recreants to come back and sign, as they could not receive their
> goods unless they signed the treaty. Away went the interpreter,
> sweating and foaming at the mouth. "Come back, oh ye rene-
> gades, and sign. You cannot receive your presents until you do
> so. Come back at once; it is only a mere matter of form."
> shouted the old man Smith.[15]

Generally the reporters, who were as anxious as Henderson to get back to the comforts of civilization, praised
Smith's efforts in getting all the Indians to sign the treaty
as well as being a valuable instrument of persuasion during the difficult situations with the hostile Cheyennes.
Unquestionably, Smith deserved a great deal of credit for
his role in the Treaty of Medicine Lodge.

When all the signings had been completed, the presents were then passed out to the Indians who carted the
goods away with great delight. The wagons which had
brought the presents, now empty, quickly headed back
for Fort Harker, while the commissioners made ready to
leave on the following morning.

That evening, however, one last spectacle took place
when the Arapahoes made a surprise visit to the camp and
conducted a farewell dance for the commissioners. The
dance lasted all night despite a heavy rain. William Fayel,
Missouri Republican correspondent, watched the dancers
at the side of John Smith, who provided an explanation of
what the various dances meant.[16]

The dances, Smith explained, were a combination of
various ceremonies then in vogue among the tribes. There
was the war dance, the chief's dance, the trader's dance,
the scalp dance, the corn dance, the dead dance, the pris-

[15] *Kansas Weekly Tribune*, Lawrence, November 14, 1867.

[16] *Missouri Republican*, November 2, 1867.

oner's dance, the return dance, the sacrifice dance, and the marriage dance. Of them all, the war dance was the most involved and entertaining. It was composed of several of the other dances, and presented an exact image of Indian war party campaigning.

First, there was represented the departure of the Indians on the war path, then the arrival of the Cheyennes in the enemy's country, the attack, the scalping of victims, the return of the victorious war party, and the torture of prisoners.

On the next day, October 29, after two weeks of camping out in the wilds of Indian country, the commissioners, the reporters, the agents, interpreters, teamsters, and others departed the council grounds at Medicine Lodge and headed across a muddy prairie for Fort Harker, arriving there as the first ice of winter was found on the Arkansas River as they crossed.

John Smith and George Bent, with their families, remained behind, however. The commissioners had given the Indians so many goods they could not begin to carry it all away, and the two interpreters took what they could to their own lodges.[17]

Medicine Lodge thus made the fourth treaty between the U.S. government and the Cheyenne and Arapaho Indians at which he had served as the official interpreter, having missed only the 1825 friendship treaty conducted by Atkinson. Medicine Lodge would be the last treaty with the Cheyennes.

[17] George Bent Letters, May 20, 1913.

12

Between Nations

Captain Smith is a man of remarkable intelligence. He assisted in revising some of the documents afterwards incorporated into Schoolcraft's voluminous works on the American Indians. Your correspondent, asking this venerable Captain where he called home, his reply was, "Wherefor my tent is pitched," pointing to a little "A" tent looming out of the snow and a little fire burning in front . . .

DeB. Randolph Keim.[1]

The Treaty of Medicine Lodge, again, settled nothing. The same basis for trouble that had existed prior to the council still controlled the destiny of the Central Plains. The old chiefs, who in the wisdom of their years saw that the old days of boundless freedom on the prairie were doomed, took their bands south of the Arkansas and established winter camps on the Cimarron and other streams in their newly assigned reserve. But the war tradition and culture of the tribes was just as strong as ever, demanding continued warfare by which the young men could win the fighting laurels that alone could give them stature and position within their tribe.

More than two thousand Cheyennes, excluding the angry bands of Medicine Arrows and Roman Nose who had refused to sign the treaty, had accepted gifts from the government at Medicine Lodge. But this by no means

---

[1] *New York Herald*, Dec. 12, 1868.

meant that the warrior societies of even the southern
camps were willing to give up their traditions of warfare
against other tribes. Only a month after Medicine Lodge a
Cheyenne and Arapaho war party engaged a group of
well-armed Kaws near Fort Zarah at the Big Bend of the
Arkansas, losing several warriors and establishing a war-
feud that would carry over to the next spring.

Furthermore, nothing really had been resolved about
the Cheyenne and Arapaho buffalo hunting grounds of
western Kansas, upon which the Indians still depended for
food as well as clothing and shelter. Henderson's last min-
ute compromise had assured that the struggle for the
buffalo land would continue once the winter was over.
With white settlements spreading across Kansas and with
increased military intrusion into what the Indians still
considered their hunting grounds, it was altogether to be
expected that future conflicts with the fight-ready Dog
Soldiers were inevitable.

On November 29, 1867, Smith came into Fort Dodge,
Kansas, with a party of eight Cheyennes, headed by
Starved Bear, and two Arapahoes from their camps forty
miles south of Dodge. He reported the Cheyennes were at
peace except for a feud with the Kiowas and were living
up to agreements made at Medicine Lodge.[2]

The peace which Medicine Lodge had sought for the
Kansas plains was further threatened by the activities of
whiskey traders who freely plied their business around
the frontier forts. Just about any buck who had a robe or
two could easily obtain firewater around Dodge or
Larned. Early in 1868 John Smith, who had been assigned
to live with the Cheyenne camps below the Arkansas and
keep a watch on them, reported to Superintendent Mur-

---

[2] Letters Sent, Fort Dodge, Captain Thompson to Captain Barr, AAG, November 29, 1867.

phy about the whiskey problem and commented that it "is certainly a dangerous thing for them to tamper with at this time."[3]

The tribes remained essentially peaceful during the winter months, though openly looking forward to spring when they could strike in revenge against the Kaws. Smith spent much of the winter with the tribes on the Cimarron, making reports to both Agent Wynkoop at Fort Larned and Superintendent Murphy on the status and feelings of Indians who complained that they had not yet received the arms and ammunition which had been promised them at Medicine Lodge. They were also disturbed by surveying parties working along the Kansas-Indian Territory border. To the Indians this meant more railroads.

On February 26, 1868, John Smith wrote to Colonel Thomas Murphy from Bull Creek where he was in camp with the Cheyennes.[4] He reported the Kiowas had robbed a party of white men of their horses on the Salt Plain in the Indian Territory, killing one man. The Cheyennes, fearing they would be blamed, requested permission to move north of the Arkansas River.

In April of 1868, Wynkoop and Smith distributed a large amount of foodstuff, including beef, bacon, flour, coffee, sugar, and salt, to the Cheyennes and Arapahoes, hoping it would help prevent the trouble which Smith warned was likely to be ahead.[5] That same month a large body of Cheyennes, possibly under Medicine Arrow and Roman Nose, and Sioux were seen hunting buffalo northwest of Fort Wallace. Since few whites knew anything about Henderson's verbal agreement with the Cheyenne

[3] Berthrong, *The Southern Cheyennes*, 300.

[4] Records of U.S. Army Command, Letters Sent, Smith to Thomas, Fort Dodge.

[5] Upper Arkansas Agency, Letters Received. Wynkoop to Murphy, Report of Distribution of Subsistence, April 10, 1868.

chiefs at Medicine Lodge, this was considered to be a treaty violation.

Meanwhile, the Cheyenne warriors from the Southern camps were still yearning for their revenge strike against the Kaws, and in late May they organized a large force of around three hundred warriors to attack a Kaw village at Council Grove, Kansas. The Kaws resisted the attack successfully in a several-hour battle, and finally the Cheyennes withdrew and rode to Fort Larned where they reported the battle to Wynkoop.

The Cheyennes blamed their lack of success with the Kaws on the better arms of their enemies and expressed, through Smith, their dissatisfaction on not getting what had been promised at Medicine Lodge.[6] They also said they fully expected to be cheated again at the scheduled mid-July annuity payment. Because of the Kaw raid, Superintendent Murphy banned the issuance of guns and ammunition to the Cheyennes, who, in turn, refused to take part in the annuity distribution and moved their camps to the Pawnee Fork.

Wynkoop convinced Commissioner Taylor on the issuance of arms and ammunition, while General Sully and Commissioner Murphy argued that further appropriations for food and clothing were necessary to keep the Indians from starving and preventing an outbreak in the fall. Accordingly, in early August Wynkoop and Smith delivered some one hundred revolvers, eight rifles, twelve kegs of powder, and 15,000 percussion caps to the Cheyennes, presumably to be used for their fall hunt.[7] Quite likely this was the true purpose for which the Cheyenne chiefs wanted them, but they were put to quite another use. In less than a week after the arms were issued, a war

---

[6] Sheridan Papers. Beecher to Sheridan, June 13, 1868.

[7] Berthrong, *The Southern Cheyennes*, 305.

party of Cheyennes plus some Sioux and Arapahoes, struck at white settlements in the Saline and Solomon valleys of western Kansas, murdering settlers, outraging and killing women, and taking several children as prisoners in addition to burning buildings and stealing stock.

The vicious attack was difficult to understand in view of the fact that the villages of the Cheyennes were vulnerably located in the Republican River area, making a planned war by the Cheyennes appear out of the question. In his report to Sheridan, Lieutenant Frederick Beecher stated that the Cheyenne warriors had come across a large amount of whiskey after suffering a defeat at the hands of the Pawnees and had fallen upon the white settlements to vent their frustration and rage.

On August 19 Colonel Wynkoop held an interview with Cheyenne Chief Little Rock at Fort Larned regarding the affair, John Smith interpreting:

Question by Colonel Wynkoop: Six nights ago I spoke to you in regard to depredations committed on the Saline. I told you to go and find out by whom these depredations were committed, and to bring me strait (sic) news. What news do you bring?

Answer by Little Rock: I took your advice and went then. I am now here to tell you all. I know this war party of Cheyennes which left the camps of their tribes above the Forks of Walnut Creek about the 2nd and 3rd of August went out against the Pawnees, crossed the Smoky Hill about Fort Hays, and thence proceeded to the Saline. There were ten (10) lodges of Sioux in the Cheyenne camp, when this war party left, and about twenty (20) men of them and four (4) Arapahoes accompanied the party, the Cheyennes numbered about two hundred (200) nearly all the young men of the village went (Little Raven's son was one of the four Arapahoes). When the party reached the Saline they turned down the stream with the exception of about twenty (20) who being fearful of depredations being committed against the whites the party going in the direction of the settlements, kept on North towards the "Pawnees" the Main party continued down the Saline until they came in sight of the settlements. They then camped where a Cheyenne named Oh-ah-moho, a brother of White Antelope who was killed at Sand Creek and another named "Red Nose" proceeded to the first house. Afterwards returned to the camp and with them a woman captive. The main party was surprised at this action and forcibly took possession of her, and returned her to her house. The two Indians outraged the women before they brought her to the camp. After the outrage had been committed the party left the Saline and went North towards the settlements of the South fork of the Solomon, where they were kindly received and fed by the white people. They left the settlements on the South fork and proceeded towards the settlements on the North fork. When in sight of these settlements they came upon a body of armed "settlers" who fired upon them. They avoided the party, went around them and approached a house some distance off. In the vicinity they came upon a white man alone upon the prairie. "Big Head's" son rode at him and knocked him down with a club. The Indian who had committed the outrage upon the white woman, known as White Antelope's Brother, then fired upon the white man without effect, while the third Indian rode up and killed him. Soon after they killed a white man and close by a woman all in the same settlement at the time these people were killed, the party was divided in feeling, the majority being opposed to any outrages being committed but judging it useless to contend against these outrages being committed without bringing on a strife among themselves, they gave way and all went together. They then went to another house in the same settlement and there killed two men, and took two little girls possession, this on the same day, after committing the last outrage the party then turned south towards the Saline where they came on a body of mounted troops. The troops immediately charged the Indians and the pursuit was continued for a long time. The Indians having the two children (their horses becoming fatigued) dropped the children without hurting them. Soon after the children were dropped the pursuit ceased but the Indians continued on up the Saline. A portion of the Indians afterwards returned to look for the children, but were unable to find them. After they had proceeded some distance up the Saline the party divided, the majority going north towards the settlements, on the Solomon, but thirty (30) of them started towards their village, supposed to be some distance Northwest of Fort Larned. Another small party returned to "Black Kettle's" village from which party I got this information. I am fearful that before this time the party that started North have committed a great many depredations. The other day when I talked with you, you gave me instructions what to do. With a great deal of risk and danger, I have followed out these instructions and returned to you with what is strait, and which I have just given you. I want you as my agent to give me advice as to what to do. I do not wish to be at war with the whites, and there are many of my nation who feel as I and who are in no way guilty, and do not wish to be punished for the bad acts of those who are guilty. We are ready and willing to abide by any advice which you may give me.

Colonel Wynkoop: Before I give you any advice, I want to ask you some questions. Do you know the names of the principal men of this party that committed the depredations besides White Antelope's Brother?

Little Rock: They were "Medicine Arrow's" oldest son named "Tall Wolf," "Red Nose" who was one of the men who outraged the woman. Big Head's son named "Porcupine Bear" and "Sand Hill's brother," known as the Bear that Goes Ahead.

Colonel Wynkoop: You told me your nation wants peace. Will you in accordance with your treaty stipulations, deliver up the men whom you have named as being the leaders of the party who committed the outrages named?

Little Rock: I think that the only men who ought to suffer and be responsible for these outrages are "White Antelope's Brother" and Red Nose, the men who ravished the woman, and when I return to the Cheyenne camps and assembly of the Chiefs and Head Men I think these two (2) men will be delivered up to you.

Colonel Wynkoop: I consider the whole party guilty, but it being impossible to punish *all* of them, I hold the principal men whom you mentioned responsible for all. They had no right to be governed and led by *two men*, if no depredations had been committed after the outrages on the woman, the two men who you have mentioned alone would have been guilty.

Little Rock: After your explanation I think your demand for

the men is right, I am willing to deliver them up, and will go back to the tribe, and use my best endeavor to have them surrendered. I am but one man and cannot answer for the entire Nation.

Colonel Wynkoop: I want you to return to your tribes and tell the Chiefs and Head Men when assembled to demand [the guilty ones given up and] tell them I think that complying with my demand is the only thing that will save their entire nation from a long and destructive war. I want you to return as soon as possible with their answer. I will see that you are safe in going and coming, and your service in this respect will be well regarded. You will be looked upon by the whites as a good man, and one who is a friend to them, as well as to his own people. And as the result of your action in this matter you will be considered by the Government as a "Great Chief," one in whom in the future they can always put the utmost confidence.

Little Rock: I am here in your service at the same time I am a "*Cheyenne*" and want to do all I can for the welfare of my Nation. If the Chiefs and Head Men refuse to comply with your demands I want to know if I can come with my wife and children (whom I love) and place myself and them under your protection. And at the same time act as a runner between you and my people?

Colonel Wynkoop: Should my demands not be complied with you can bring your lodge and family here and I will protect you.[8]

Severely dismayed following another Cheyenne raid along the Arkansas valley in Colorado on September 8, Wynkoop asked for a leave of absence from his agency and returned to Philadelphia. The feelings he expressed relative to the recent Cheyenne outbreak were the same as felt by John Smith: the massacre at Sand Creek, the burning of the Cheyenne village by Hancock, the inadequate time given the chiefs to surrender young men guilty

[8] Bureau of Indian Affairs, Cheyenne and Arapaho Indians. Interview between Col. E. W. Wynkoop, U.S. Indian Agent and Little Rock, a Cheyenne Chief, held at Fort Larned, Kansas, August 19, 1868.

of crimes, the failure of Congress to appropriate enough supplies, and the punishment of innocent Indians for the crimes of the guilty made peace with the Indians virtually impossible.

Superintendent Murphy, disillusioned by the outbreaks, sided with General Sherman in believing that the Cheyennes and Arapahoes deserved to be hunted down by the army and punished until they sued for peace. Further incidents soon took place adding support to the military view, the most important of which was the famous Beecher Island fight.

After two scouts had been attacked, one of them killed and another seriously wounded, by Cheyennes on the Solomon River, General Sheridan ordered his aide, Major Forsyth, to form a striking force composed of fifty frontier scouts. Lieutenant Beecher joined the unit also. In September the unit left Fort Wallace and trailed a raiding party up the Arikaree fork where they camped on September 16. There they were attacked by a large force of Cheyennes and driven to a small sandbar in the dry bed of the Arikaree where they held off the Indians until help reached them on the morning of September 25.

Killed in the action was Lieutenant Beecher, Dr. John Mooers, surgeon, and four of the scouts. The Indian losses were, as usual, indeterminable, Forsyth claiming thirty-two killed while the Indians said only nine of their force were killed. It is certain, however, that among their losses was the famous Cheyenne war leader, Roman Nose.

On October 11 Tall Bull's Dog Soldiers attacked a Fifth Cavalry scouting force on the Republican, killing two troopers, while only a few days earlier a force of Cheyennes and Arapahoes attacked a wagon train near the mouth of Sand Creek on the Arkansas River, capturing Mrs. Clara Blinn and her small child. Other engagements between troops and Indians occurred, and it had become increasingly clear that the war which the Medicine Lodge council had interrupted was now renewed in earnest.

Wynkoop's absence from the Plains left John Smith without employment or base. And with the war sect in control among the Cheyennes, he was no longer welcome or safe in their camps. Smith's great experience and knowledge of the country were quickly put to use, however, by Brevet Brigadier General Alfred Sully, commanding the Military District of the Upper Arkansas, who on September 7 marched from Fort Dodge southward to hunt for and attack the Cheyennes along the Cimarron and North Canadian Rivers of Indian Territory.[9] Also along as scouts were Ben Clark and Amos Chapman, who, like Smith, were married into the Cheyenne tribe.

After scouting without success along Crooked Creek in southwestern Kansas, Sully's command dropped on southward to the Cimarron, with four companies of the Seventh Cavalry, under Major Elliott, scouting ahead. Although the troops found plenty of Indian sign, it wasn't until the 10th of September that the advance guard of Smith, Clark, and Chapman was attacked by Cheyennes. The troops killed two Indians, driving them off, but during the night Sully's camp was surrounded, and on the morning of the 11th Indians captured two straggling troopers of the rear guard. Captain Louis Hamilton, who commanded the rear guard, pursued the Indians and eventually forced them to release the two captives. One of the troopers was killed and the other wounded severely.

Sully continued his march down the Cimarron, harassed all the way by Cheyenne Dog Soldiers from the sagebrush hills along the river who not only were armed with repeating rifles but signalled to one another with bugle

---

[9] Berthrong, *The Southern Cheyennes*, 318.

calls. The march progressed into a running fight with the soldiers killing several Indians. Finally, the Cheyennes took a stand on some high ground along Beaver Creek in northwestern Indian Territory. Sully dismounted and fought on foot until the Indians slipped away under cover of decoys and false trails.

Sully continued his pursuit along the North Canadian past the mouth of Wolf Creek and caught up with the Indians once more in the sand hills just to the east. There he dismounted once more and found himself neatly bogged down and in danger of losing his baggage train. On September 14, Sully gave up his hopes of finding the elusive Cheyenne encampment and ordered a return to Fort Dodge.

The Cheyenne warriors escorted them out of the Indian Territory at a distance, making derisive signs of thumbing their noses and smacking their rumps.

It was these two affairs—the Beecher Island defeat and Sully's inept campaign into Indian Territory—which convinced Generals Sherman and Sheridan that a major campaign would be necessary to punish the Cheyennes and force them to accept a lasting peace. A plan was devised whereby a refuge for the "old, young, and feeble" would be established at Fort Cobb in the southern part of Indian Territory while the army conducted punitive operations against the hostiles.

It was a similar policy to the one supposedly attempted by Evans and Chivington in Colorado, and ironically it would have the same disastrous and undeserved results for the most peaceful-natured of the Cheyennes who comprised the village of Cheyenne Chief Black Kettle. John Smith saw it coming, but even his warning to the Indians was not enough to overcome the fateful course of history.

13

Beware the Washita

John Smith, the interpreter, thinks they [the Cheyennes and Arapahoes] will endeavor to capture along the Salina and Solomon and between Fort Harker and Council Grove a number of whites to exchange for the fifty-three Indian women and children now in our hands.

Leavenworth Times and Conservative.[1]

Sheridan's war plans involved a coordinated attack against the Indians in western Oklahoma and the Texas Panhandle from three directions: from Fort Bascom in New Mexico along the South Canadian River; from Fort Lyon southeastward along the upper Beaver and Wolf Creeks; and southward from a supply base in northwestern Oklahoma. Meanwhile, efforts were made to "talk in" the friendly-disposed Indians. Brevet Major General William M. Hazen was assigned to the job of meeting with the Kiowas and Comanches at Fort Larned on September 20, 1868. There he promised to conduct the Indians to Fort Cobb in the Indian Territory personally.

When the Kiowas and Comanches failed to meet at Larned as promised, the blame was placed squarely on John Smith.

The Kiowas and Yapparikas unite in saying that one John Smith, interpreter, first led them to break their appointment with General Hazen, by telling them that the General would not come as he had promised, thru fear of an attack from the Chey-

---

[1] *Leavenworth Times and Conservative*, Jan. 19, 1869.

ennes; that the same Smith afterwards told them they had better move south and west rapidly, not going to either Larned or Cobb, as the Military had set traps for them at both places.[2]

The peaceable Cheyennes under Black Kettle evidently were advised by Smith in the same fashion, for they, too, left the Arkansas and Cimarron in the fall and moved on further southward to the Washita River of west central Oklahoma and went into camp with the Arapahoes, Comanches, and Kiowas. Here they felt reasonably safe. The area was well removed from white settlements and transportation routes, and no U.S. troops had ever penetrated the region in force.

But to further protect his tribe, Black Kettle rode nearly a hundred miles from his camp to Fort Cobb, where on November 20 he met with Captain Henry Alvord and General Hazen, who had himself just arrived. Black Kettle said that his village of 180 lodges wanted peace and professed no control over other Cheyenne bands. Hazen, knowing Sheridan's war plans, declined Black Kettle's peace offer and further refused to allow them to come into Fort Cobb. But he did allow Black Kettle to return to his Washita encampment thinking that he was safe from attack from the military.

Hazen was much incensed at Smith about his advice to the Indians, reporting to Sherman that "This man, John Smith, referred to and others at Larned, seem to be self constituted authorities in all Indian matters."[3] And later, he wrote, "This is a part of the advice given them by John Smith and other Indian men on the Arkansas. The influence of these men is always bad."[4]

---

[2] Sheridan Papers, Report of Captain Henry E. Alvord, Fort Cobb, IT, November 5, 1868.

[3] Hazen to Sherman, November 7, 1868, Fort Cobb.

[4] Hazen to Sherman, November 10, 1868, Fort Cobb.

Meanwhile, Sheridan's plans were rapidly getting under way. Even as Black Kettle was on his way back to his Washita camps, General Sully, guided by John Smith, left Fort Dodge under orders by Sheridan to return to the vicinity of the North Canadian River and find a suitable location for a supply post.

Sully's command included eleven companies of Seventh Cavalry under Brevet Major General George A. Custer. The unit's officer corps listed such names as Brevet Lieutenant Colonel M. W. Keogh, Major Joel H. Elliott, Brevet Lieutenant Colonel Frederick W. Benteen, Brevet Captain Thomas W. Custer, Lieutenant Louis M. Hamilton, and Lieutenant Myles Moylan, many of whom would still be in Custer's command eight years later at the Little Big Horn.

Additionally, there were three companies of Third Infantry, one of Fifth Infantry, one of the Thirty-Eighth Infantry, and a train of some 450 wagons. General Sully commanded the train, and the expedition followed essentially the same course as two months earlier. The wagons were organized four abreast to be less exposed to attack. An advance guard of two companies of cavalry rode ahead while two more guarded the rear.

Early on the morning of November 11, 1868, the long column of mounted troops and wagons departed Fort Dodge and marched eastward down the north bank of the Arkansas for some eight miles. They rose at sunrise on the twelfth, crossed the Arkansas, and began their march southeasterly across ". . . rolling plains, covered with buffalo grass, no trees, and broken into ravines," crossing Mulberry Creek where they encamped on the twelfth. On the thirteenth they followed a ridge near Bluff Creek until two in the afternoon when they made camp after twenty and one-half miles had been registered on their odometer

for the day's trek. Six buffalo had been killed during the
march despite a thick fog which had clung to the surrounding countryside most of the day. Keim's account in
the *Herald* gives an excellent word picture of a typical
military march and its problems:

> November 14—Left camp at a quarter past six this morning.
> Marched one and a half miles to Bluff Creek. The crossing of the
> creek was found to be very difficult. The creek bed was about
> 200 yards wide, with a sedgy island in the middle, with a sand
> bed about thirty feet wide. On the south side are bluffy banks,
> with very bad descents for wagons. Plenty of cottonwood timber
> on this side. After crossing ascended the bluffs winding up the
> bed of a small ravine, reaching a divide which was followed for
> five miles. From this point descended into a basin in which was
> very fine grass and the dry sand bed of a creek tending towards
> the Cimarron. This basin was one and a half miles in width.
> Across this basin the line of march lay towards the summit of
> another ridge. From the crest of this ridge the country made a
> gradual descent to Bear Creek. This bottom land is four or five
> miles wide, with the creek running through the middle. Crossed
> the creek above the forks. The crossings are both bad on account
> of the steepness of the banks. The first fork is fifty feet in width
> and the second 130, with sand beds. The first has water in pools.
> The column camped on the first fork, making fourteen and a
> quarter miles. Water good, grass fair and very little timber.[5]

By the fifteenth, Sully's force had reached the Cimarron, and here at about noon a violent norther struck,
lasting all day and the ensuing night. Major Joel Elliott
was sent on with a force of cavalry and infantry and the
heaviest wagons with instructions to march to the Beaver
and make a dry camp. The rest of the command and
Elliott's command reunited on the Beaver on the sixteenth, with the weather now turned extremely cold.

Sully continued down the south bank of the Beaver and
on the eighteenth struck its juncture with Wolf Creek,

---

[5] *New York Herald*, December 12, 1868.

where only two months before he had fought the Cheyenne Dog Soldiers. Here they crossed the trail of a war party headed north, estimated by Smith to be seventy-five strong and about two days old, and camped on the south bank of Wolf Creek, three miles below its confluence with the Beaver.

On the nineteenth Sully ordered a scouting of the adjacent country to search for a site for the supply post. It would need to possess the requisites of enough wood, water, and winter grass for a large command and to be within one hundred miles of Fort Dodge.

> On November 19 a thorough reconnaissance was made of the adjacent country and the result was entirely satisfactory in view of the objects in view. The site selected for the proposed post is immediately on the confluence of the Beaver River and Wolf Creek, which, united here, form the main fork of the Canadian.[6]

Keim gives full credit to John Smith for selection of the site of what came to be known as Camp Supply.

> Connected with the selection of this admirable site I must not omit to give credit to the person to whom all is due. That person is John Simpson Smith, an old plainsman, over sixty years of age . . . His familiarity with this region at once pointed him out as a suitable person to direct the line of march to some suitable locality. For this purpose General Sully secured the services which the old man, though far advanced in years, felt it his duty to extend. General Sheridan expresses himself perfectly satisfied with the site.[7]

The expedition had no sooner arrived at Camp Supply than a quarrel developed between Sully and Custer over whether or not to await the arrival of the Nineteenth Kansas Volunteers, under Governor S. J. Crawford, who had become lost on the way. They were also arguing over who would be the field commander of the troops. This was quickly resolved by General Sheridan, who arrived at

---

[6] *Ibid.*   [7] *Ibid.*

Supply on the twenty-first. Sheridan, preferring Custer to direct field operations, sent Sully back to Fort Harker, and ordered Custer to move against the Indians in the direction of the Washita River and attack them wherever he found them.[8]

A snow storm struck the new post on the night of November 22, but despite well over a foot accumulation by morning, Custer led the eleven companies of Seventh Cavalry out of Camp Supply at daybreak on the twenty-third, the regimental band playing the lilting "The Girl I Left Behind Me."

John Smith and General Custer still had no use for one another, and Smith was having none of Custer's Indian hunting. He knew full well what had happened at Sand Creek and he smelled another massacre in the air. Thus John Smith remained behind at Camp Supply as the Seventh headed southward toward the Washita.

Custer marched his command southwestward down Wolf Creek, tracing the same route that Major John Sedgwick and Lieutenant J. E. B. Stuart had followed when they were looking for Kiowas and Comanches before the Civil War in 1860.[9] With such heavy snow on the ground and the weather so cold, Custer's troops found the Wolf Creek Valley flooded with game and while waiting for the wagons to catch up, Custer took his two wolf hounds and enjoyed a buffalo hunt.

On the fifth day, after four marches and campings on Wolf Creek, Custer turned his command directly southward towards where the Antelope Hills stand just south of the South Canadian River and just east of the 100th meridian which marked the boundary of Indian Territory

---

[8] *New York Herald*, December 2, 1868.

[9] Kiowa-Comanche Campaign of 1860, *Kansas Historical Quarterly*, vol. 23, 1957. Stuart's Diary refers to Wolf Creek as "Middle Creek."

and the Texas Panhandle. Upon reaching the Canadian, Custer sent Elliott on ahead with three troops of cavalry to hunt for Indian signs. Meanwhile he began moving his white-topped wagons across the river and up to high ground at a crossing near the Antelope Hills. Custer himself rode to the top of one of the five plateaus which towered above the plains to view the "immense circle of snowy whiteness" and from there he saw Elliott's courier coming in to report that the scout troops had found a fresh Indian trail leading southward.

Custer took all but eighty men, whom he left with the baggage train, and cut across country to join Elliott late on the evening of November 26. After only an hour's rest, to eat and drink coffee, Custer ordered his troops back into their saddles and by moonlight proceeded to follow the trail eastward down the Washita.

The New York Daily Tribune printed an account of the march, as written by someone listed as an "Occasional Correspondent," probably an officer in the Seventh:

> It was after midnight, when two Osage Indian scouts in the advance, announced that they smelt the smoke of a wood fire, a fire which we came upon after going about a mile further. Around it were the traces of Indian boys who had been herding ponies. On we pushed again, the crisp-frozen snow rustling softly under the horses' feet, and our long, dark column winding through the valley like a huge black monster. Not a voice could be heard. Then miles more were passed, and the scouts, who were ascending elevated ground, suddenly wheeled their horses and quickly moved to the rear, reporting that ponies were grazing nearly a mile ahead of us, and that a village was doubtless in the woods beyond, which skirts the stream in the valley. Strict silence was observed, not one white man who looked, could, by the utmost straining of the eyes, see a living object where the telescopic vision of those Indian scouts had discovered so much. Soon a night-glass verified the presence of the animals. The officers were assembled by General Custer, and all cautiously

crept up to the crest of the hill overlooking the valley below, and the surroundings were all carefully noted. It was a moment of exultation, and the General's enthusiastic instructions were quickly and eagerly given and received.[10]

Custer divided the Seventh Cavalry troops into four detachments and surrounded the village, removing all sabres to prevent any noise to disturb the frozen stillness of the snowy prairie. No fires were permitted, and the men sat around and talked in muffled tones about the impending battle or followed Custer in spreading themselves on the snow for a rest. Finally the cold, gray dawn broke, and as Custer was about to give the signal for attack, a shot was fired on the far side of camp.

Immediately Custer ordered the bugle to sound the charge and, as the regimental band played Garry Owen, some eight hundred mounted soldiers galloped down upon the unsuspecting village of Cheyenne chief Black Kettle. It was the morning of November 27, 1868—almost four years to the day after the Colorado troops under Colonel John M. Chivington had struck Black Kettle's camp at Sand Creek.

Again the Cheyenne camp reacted as best it could, the men dashing from the lodges some with guns, some with bows and arrows, attempting to fight off the troops long enough for the women, children, and old ones to escape. Some were killed immediately, Black Kettle among them, but many made it to the shelter of trees and sand embankments from which they began to put up an effective counterfire. Many of the women and children dashed for whatever place of hiding they could find, but could do nothing more than cower inside their lodges.

The troops quickly gained control of the village area, as it became a melee of charging horses, yelling cavalrymen,

[10] *New York Daily Tribune*, December 29, 1868.

and rifle smoke. Unable to drive the warriors from the positions, Custer dismounted his men and fought on foot, finally working above the sharpshooting Indians, and dislodging them. Inside the lodges the Cheyenne squaws began their death chant.

One group of Cheyenne women and children were being led to escape by Chief Little Rock, but they were spotted by Major Elliott who led some fifteen soldiers in pursuit. This was the last time Elliott or the men were seen alive by their comrades. Lieutenant Hamilton had been shot near the heart and killed during the initial charge.

Custer ordered the Indian lodges pulled down, and when all of the captured property had been placed into a pile, it was burned. Units of the Seventh Cavalry had captured the Cheyenne horseherd, and, fearing a counterattack from the mounted warriors who now ringed the encampment, Custer ordered the ponies shot, some 875 of them.

As with most fights between white soldiers and Indians, the number of killed and wounded is subject to dispute. Custer reported 103 Indians killed, warriors he claimed, and 53 squaws and children taken as prisoners, while he lost two officers and nineteen enlisted men.

Custer sent out parties to search for Elliott and his men, but after looking for about two miles they returned, fearing they would be cut off. The Indians on the perimeter of the field continued to grow in numbers, though they could not fire on the troops for fear of hitting the prisoners. Throwing skirmishers out, with colors flying and the band playing, Custer put his blue-coated columns in march toward the Indian villages below on the Washita. As he hoped, this caused the warriors surrounding him much consternation and sent them downriver to protect their camps. Custer continued his bluff until well after dark, then reversed back past the battleground, rejoined his wagon train, and headed back toward Camp Supply.

When John Smith's Cheyenne wife Na-to-mah learned that Custer had massacred the Cheyennes on the Washita, she tried to kill herself, first with a knife and then by swallowing strychnine. A Kansas doctor, however, saved her life in both instances.[11] The news of Black Kettle's death was a severe blow to Smith. Black Kettle, and many of the other murdered Cheyennes, were life-long friends. Smith knew, too, that the strongest voice for peace among the Cheyennes was dead at the hands of Custer.

Wynkoop had been the peacemaker for the whites; Black Kettle for the Cheyennes. And John Smith had been their instrument. Now they were both gone, and it was too late to save the Cheyenne. As Custer and Sheridan quickly reoutfitted and headed the Seventh southward again on December 7, Smith knew that the days of freedom on the Plains were ended for the tribes. The force of white men was too much for even the Cheyenne warrior.

Custer and Sheridan revisited the Washita battlefield, found the bodies of Elliott and his men, plus that of a white woman and her child who had been captives of the Cheyennes and were murdered during the fight. Going on to Fort Cobb, Sheridan talked with a Cheyenne delegation led by Little Robe of the Cheyennes and Yellow Bear of the Arapahoes, who later surrendered their tribes at newly established Fort Sill in January of 1869.

Most of the Cheyennes still refused to come in, and the military still blamed it on John Smith's warning that Fort Cobb was a trap. But it wasn't until March that Custer took eleven companies of the Seventh, plus ten companies

[11] Charles J. Brill, *Conquest of the Southern Plains* (Oklahoma City: Golden Saga Publishers, 1938), 313–14.

of the 19th Kansas Volunteers, and marched into the Texas Panhandle, where on the Sweetwater he found the Cheyenne Dog Soldiers under Medicine Arrow and Little Robe. Capturing four of the Cheyenne chiefs, Custer secured the release of two white women from the Cheyennes but took three of the chiefs back to Camp Supply as hostages to bring the tribes in.

Though the chiefs were later taken to Fort Hays where two of them were killed trying to escape, finally in April, 1869, Little Robe and some other chiefs arrived at Fort Sill with 67 lodges. The Dog Soldiers were given the choice by Little Robe of agreeing to live on the reservation or leaving the country. The Dogs, under Tall Bull and White Horse, brandished their guns against the sky and claimed that they ". . . had always been a free nation, and they would remain so or die." Na-to-mah reported that 165 lodges of Dog Soldiers had discarded their lodges and had left Little Robe's camp and headed north where their battle for survival could continue.[12]

The remaining Cheyennes now began to arrive at Camp Supply, where Smith and George Bent were interpreters, their arrival coinciding with a new peace policy initiated by President Grant. This policy involved the entrusting of the Southern tribes of Plains Indians to the Society of Friends, bringing about the establishment of the Upper Arkansas Agency at Camp Supply during the summer of 1869.

With the hostiles gone north and a tentative peace once more established with the Southern bands of the Cheyenne, John Smith could now return to his old service as an interpreter for the military and the Indian Bureau and as a trader, this time for C. F. Tracy and Company, who held the trading monopoly at Camp Supply.

---

[12] Berthrong, *The Southern Cheyennes*, 340.

14

The Odyssey Ends

On the 29th of 6th mo., 1871, John S. Smith, late U.S. Ind. Interpreter for Cheyennes and Arapahoes, deceased, and left some considerable amount of property, which has been placed in my possession until some legal steps are taken to administer upon his affairs. His property consists of 1 pair of Black Horses; 1 set Double Harness; 1 Spring Wagon; $216 in currency; 2 trunks containing clothing, Jewelry, etc.; 2 Valises containing clothing, Jewelry, etc.; 1 Revolving Pistol and holster; 1 old cook stove; a set dishes. . .

Agent Brinton Darlington.[1]

Smith was at Camp Supply on May 25, 1869, when Brevet Lieutenant Colonel A. D. Nelson arrived there and began issuing annuity goods to some 1,320 Indians, representing 257 lodges. The rations, hauled down from Kansas by wagon caravan, were unloaded into separate piles, and the younger chiefs doled out the goods to a huge circle of women and children who waited patiently for their turn. After the goods were all distributed, Nelson asked Smith to call the head men into council.

Through the interpreter, Nelson told the chiefs that they would have to return to the region north of the Cimarron, where they had been assigned by the Treaty of Medicine Lodge. But the Indians were adamant in their opposition to this. The ground there, they said, was so

---

[1] Cheyenne and Arapaho Letter Book, Darlington to Hoag, July 15, 1871.

covered with salt that it looked like snow, and the water in the streams so brackish that their horses would not drink it. Also they wanted very much to be further from the Osage reserve in southeastern Kansas. The Osages, they claimed, raided their camps and stole their horses. They much preferred to stay on the Beaver and Wolf Creeks west of Camp Supply.[2]

During the summer and fall of 1869, the military continued to issue goods to the Indians from Camp Supply. In September some three-thousand Indians were issued 18,-270 pounds of bacon and 195,710 pounds of shelled corn, which Little Raven complained was so bad even his horses wouldn't eat it. Herds of Texas Longhorn cattle were also purchased, but for their meat the Indians much preferred to hunt the buffalo which were still plentiful in the Territory that year.[3]

Kiowa chief, Satanta, appeared at the post requesting food. He was told to go to Medicine Bluff Creek Ft. Sill for supplies, but he said that he had already been there and all he had been given was some dry meal which he couldn't eat. Not long afterwards a herd of 128 beeves suddenly stampeded and disappeared from the Supply area. John Smith blamed the Kiowas for running off the cattle.[4]

One of the big problems connected with the issue of beef to the Indians involved the matter of hides. These were of much value to the military, but cow hides meant nothing to the Indian bucks, who delighted in killing the cows by chasing them as if they were buffalo and filling

---

[2] Fort Supply Letter Book, Nelson from Fort Supply, May 28, 1869.

[3] *Ibid.*, Bonney to Morgan, August 14, 1869.

[4] *Ibid.*, December 28, 1869.

them full of bullet and arrow holes. To prevent the hides from being ruined, it was necessary for the soldiers to slaughter the cattle for the Indians.[5]

Another problem arose when Captain Seth Bonney attempted to erect a shelter to house the tribal supplies. When he went to Arapaho chief Little Raven and suggested that he would like to hire some braves to help cut timber and haul logs, he soon learned an interesting fact about wild Plains Indians. "Indian don't know how to work," Little Raven told him. "Gets tired too quick." Only the Indian women knew about work, and Bonney considered even hiring some of them but decided against it.[6]

In July 1869, a new agent for the Cheyennes and Arapahoes had arrived in Indian Territory. He was Quaker Brinton Darlington who, though in his sixties and completely without experience with Indians, was thoroughly honest and devoted to the fulfillment of his new task. Knowing absolutely nothing about Indians and just as uncertain about what his new assignment involved, Darlington arrived at Pond Creek, a tributary of the Salt Fork of the Arkansas, and constructed two log cabins and dug a well. This was only a short distance east of the Great Salt Plains and precisely the place which his new charges, the Cheyennes and Arapahoes, wished to avoid.

Visiting Camp Supply on August 11, 1869, Darlington learned to his surprise that one of his duties was to issue the annuity goods to the tribes. Having absolutely no idea as to how this was done he soon "called to my assistance Geo. Bent and John S. Smith, Interpreters, who carefully

---

[5] *Ibid.*, October 1, 1869.

[6] Upper Arkansas Agency, Letters Received, Darlington to Parker, August 13, 1869.

explained to them (the Arapaho chiefs) first the contents of the order relating to rations."[7]

When President Grant signed an executive order relocating the two tribes on lands south and west of the Cimarron, Darlington made a tour of the country south of Supply and found a suitable site for his agency on the North Canadian River where it was crossed by the Fort Harker-Fort Sill military road. Everyone was in agreement that the abundant water and grass there, plus its nearness to the new reserve area, made it an ideal location.

The Cheyennes, however, were still recalcitrant about accepting reservation life, and during the winter of 1869–70 only a few of them reported in. In November, 1869, a council was called by Darlington near Camp Supply. Through Smith, Bull Bear and a group of warriors assured the Quaker agent that with each passing day the Cheyennes were feeling better towards the white man.

The Dog Soldier leader also requested that Darlington seek the release of some Cheyennes who had been captured by white troops in the north. But the Cheyennes were still suspicious of the agency because of the presence of white troops so close by at Supply. Because of this, Darlington was prompted once again to move his agency, and on May 3, 1870, located it even further east on the North Canadian River, just west of present-day Oklahoma City.[8]

Though some of the Arapahoes followed, only a few Cheyenne lodges—those of Stone Calf, George Bent, and John Smith—were with Darlington when he arrived at what was later to be known as the Darlington Agency.

---

[7] Darlington Agency, Letters Sent, Darlington to Hoag, Camp Supply, September 1, 1869.

[8] Berthrong, *The Southern Cheyennes*, 355.

Smith was named the official interpreter for the post at $400 per annum. Records indicate that he and his Indian wife also drew beef issues along with the Indians.[9]

A sawmill was transported from Kansas, and the first agency buildings were erected. Two-hundred twenty acres of virgin prairie were broken and planted in vegetables and grain. During the spring and summer of 1870, bands of both the Arapaho and Cheyenne tribes dropped by the agency to camp and receive rations, but they soon returned to the buffalo range of western Oklahoma which was still free from the dominance of the white man and where they could still live the old life.

There was, in fact, a great deal of resentment among the tribes against those who took up the white man's road. Strangely, it was Arapaho chief Big Mouth, who had led the Arapaho force which killed Elliott at the Washita and who now rode the Major's horse, who was first among the Indians to go against tribal pressure. He began farming eighty acres at Darlington Agency, eighteen of them in corn.[10]

In November of 1870, a small group of Quaker officials made a buggy-tour of the still-wild Indian Territory, going from Tahlequah in the northeastern corner all the way to Fort Sill in the far southwestern corner. They arrived at the Darlington Agency in late November and spent the Thanksgiving holiday there. With the work routine suspended, a meeting was held Thanksgiving morning to give thanks and sermons were delivered by the Quakers. Later a council was held with Big Mouth, White Crow, and Yellow Horse of the Arapahoes and Little Robe, who had

---

[9] Oklahoma State Historical Society, Indian Archives, Cheyenne and Arapaho Files, Employees, Receipt for Services, signed by John S. Smith, March 31, 1871.

[10] Cheyenne and Arapaho Letters, Report to Dr. Nicholson, August 7, 1871, Oklahoma Historical Society.

taken over as principal chief of the Cheyennes following Black Kettle's death. John Smith did the interpreting as the Indians stated the reluctance of their tribes to take up the white man's road.[11]

On another occasion, Cheyenne chief Red Moon explained through Smith that the tribes were very unhappy about a prohibition placed in the issuing of ammunition. They wished to be able to move about and hunt, and they expressed their dislike of the railroads which always brought more white men onto their lands.[12]

Smith, however, did not spend all his time at Darlington. Despite the fact that he was now in his sixties, he still made the long rides in his wagon to where the bands were camped along Wolf Creek, the Beaver, and other streams of western Oklahoma. He went in part for the agency and in part as a trader. Darlington found Smith's trading activities as one way of satisfying their complaints about the lack of supplies. But Smith was still suspect to the military and other frontier whites. A letter written on March 23, 1871, from Camp Supply complains of the "unprincipled interpreters" who mislead the government concerning the Indians:

> Take old John Smith for instance. I have heard him say very mysteriously a few days since he "anticipated more trouble this summer than anyone was aware of." Next day Little Robe and some others came in for rations and John got some 90 robes from them for Thompson and Hills. He immediately came to us glowing with the information that "since he was with the Cheyennes he never found them so friendly or well disposed as this season." Again he told Mr. Darlington by whom he is also employed that "the military were bound to bring on a war any-

---

[11] William Nicholson, "A Tour of Indian Agencies in Kansas and the Indian Territory in 1870," *The Kansas Historical Quarterly*, vol. III (November, 1934), 348.

[12] *Ibid.*, 349.

how." Same day he informed Captain Schindel "we were certain of trouble—he knew it all along."[13]

The contradiction of Smith's reports, however, was by no means unexplainable, for the chiefs themselves were hot and cold on their situation in the Indian Territory. To the south the Kiowas and Comanches had resumed their raiding into Texas, and some of the young men of the Cheyenne had ridden with them. The period of the seventies in Indian Territory would be characterized by a constant suspicion of one another by the principals involved in the early reservation period of the Cheyenne and Arapaho tribes.

The Indians were suspicious and distrustful of the military, though they came gradually to like and accept the honest Darlington. The military was wary of the Indians, the Indian Bureau, and the old frontier whites such as Smith who were associated with the tribes. It was a dangerous situation that desperately needed a stabilizing solution.

In the spring of 1871, principally at the suggestion of Little Raven, it was decided that a visit by the chiefs of the two tribes to Washington, D.C., might help the cause of peace. A delegation was made up for that purpose, consisting of Little Raven, Bird Chief, and Powder Face of the Arapahoes; Little Robe and Stone Calf of the Cheyennes; and Buffalo Goad of the Wichitas. The Cheyennes requested that Philip McCusker be taken as their interpreter, but he did not speak the Arapaho tongue fluently and Little Raven requested that John Smith be taken as their interpreter.[14]

[13] Letters Received, Central Superintendency, March 23, 1871, from F.P. Cleary, Camp Supply.

[14] Darlington to Enoch Hoag, May 4, 1871, Central Agency.

Leaving from Camp Supply, the delegation party arrived in Washington in mid-May, making the third delegation visit for Smith and his fourth official trip to the
nation's capitol. Smith's friend, Colonel A. G. Tracy,
trader at Fort Dodge, was in Washington and acted as a
guide in escorting the chiefs to places of interest. The
Indians visited the Naval Yards and the capitol buildings,
including the White House where they were so over-
awed with the rotunda and the paintings there that they
refused to believe they were man-made.

Meeting with the Commissioner of Indian Affairs
Parker, Buffalo Goad laid his feelings emphatically on the
line:

"Here I am," he said, "with a white man's coat and
pantaloons on, but there are no 'greenbacks' in my
pocket, and now I hope the Government will give me
some to carry around, so as to show something for the
lands that have been taken."[15]

On May 23rd the chiefs were taken to visit President
Grant, who asked them about recent troubles on the
Texas border. Smith explained for the chiefs that the trouble was caused mainly by young Kiowas. Upon leaving the
president, the chiefs were taken to the Treasury Department, where they became much alarmed and frightened
upon seeing an elevator in the building, scattering in all
directions.[16]

On the night before leaving, the delegation was taken
to a YMCA meeting, where they were placed on the stage
as honored guests. They heard the assembly sing "From
Greenland's Icy Mountains" and listened to an introduc-
tory speech by General O. O. Howard. When asked to
speak to the group, Buffalo Goad again bared his thoughts
on the Indian's situation:

---

[15] *New York Times*, May 23, 1871.   [16] *Ibid.*, May 24, 1871.

"This country was given to the Indian, and when white man came, Indian helped him; now white man rich. Indian poor." He said he did not know how this was, unless it was from the better medicine of the white man, and he now wanted to take the white man's medicine.[17]

Though the chiefs desired to get home the quickest way possible, they were routed through Philadelphia, New York City, and Boston. On June 1st the *New York Times* reported that the Indians had been in town for several days, quietly sight-seeing in "European clothes." They visited Central Park where they saw so many strange animals that Little Raven commented: "My eyes saw more than they could carry." The chiefs were taken to the harbor where they could see boat loads of immigrants arriving and were told, with questionable diplomacy, that because of all these new arrivals more room would be needed out West. The chiefs were crestfallen.[18] Later, they were guests at a big rally in Cooper's Union, where before a huge audience John Smith interpreted remarks made by the Indian chiefs.[19]

From New York the delegation moved on to Boston. Following a reception held at Tremont Temple, they took carriage rides around the city, visiting the capitol and meeting the governor of the state and mayor of Boston. From Boston the delegation was taken to Philadelphia. Though the plan had originally been to return via St. Louis, another change of itinerary was made, and the group was taken by railroad car to Chicago. Here, on June 9th, they were guests of honor at a meeting in Farwell Hall. During the Chicago meeting which was sponsored by the Peace Commission, the chiefs were introduced to a crowd of some twelve hundred persons. Sena-

---

[17] *Ibid.*, May 25, 1871.   [18] *Ibid.*, June 1, 1871.

[19] *Ibid.*, June 2, 1871.

tor Doolittle and other governmental figures made speeches, and through Smith Little Raven responded with a few words. He humorously commented that since the chiefs had been given horses in Philadelphia, they would not have to walk home. Afterwards the band played Yankee Doodle, and the audience passed before the Indians and interpreters to view them more closely.[20]

John Smith was introduced to the crowd as a "resident of the plains for the past 40 years," but the newspaper accounts gave no clue as to the old plainsman's health. It is likely that he was already feeling the effects of the tiring trip and had, perhaps, already developed the early stages of pneumonia. Within twenty days of the Chicago meeting, John Smith was back in his Indian lodge at the Darlington Agency where on June 29, 1871, at the age of 61 he died in his blankets.[21] He was buried among a grove of trees one-half mile west of the agency on the banks of the North Canadian River.

Smith's possessions were all given up by his Cheyenne wife, Na-to-mah, for the benefit of young William Gilpin Smith, known as "Willie," who was then attending school near Lawrence, Kansas, under the care of a Quaker family. Smith had placed him there with the request that he should not again go among the Indians. Na-to-mah later came back to the agency, stayed for a time, then claimed the horses and went out with the tribe.[22]

It was discovered by Darlington that Smith also held patents to two sections of land in Colorado for young Willie and for his daughter Armana, who was now married and living to the north among the Sioux.[23] The funds

---

[20] *Chicago Tribune*, June 10, 1871.

[21] Cheyenne and Arapaho Agency Files, Darlington to Hoag, July 15, 1871.

[22] *Ibid.*, Darlington to Hoag, January 1, 1872.

[23] *Ibid.*

from Smith's estate, $609.96, were sent to Lawrence for Willie's education.[24]

A short time after Smith's death, Darlington received two interesting letters relating to the frontiersman. One, forwarded through the German Consul, was from a New York woman named Miller who had read of Smith's visit to New York City in the papers.[25] She believed that he might well have been her long lost brother who had gone to live among the Indians thirty or forty years before. The boy, she said, had been a drummer boy in Germany and had had the lapel of his ear slit for an earring. Further, his father had been a button-maker, and the boy had been trained in that profession. Darlington supplied what information he knew, but despite certain similarities between Smith's early history and the one described by Mrs. Miller, a second letter seemed to pretty well prove otherwise.

This letter was forwarded to Darlington from Camp Supply:

> Colonel I. W. Davis, St. Louis August 4th, 1871. Dear Sir ex-cuse me for takeing the liberty to ask of you information of my brother John S. Smith, Indian Interpreter for Cheyenne & Arap-ahoes. I read in the papers here he died a few days after he arrived home from Washington. I was most unfortunate after years of waiting, I expected to see him on his way home—but in Chicago the Indian Delegation was ordered to move on another route—Death has taken my Brother & I am left alone—I tried to get information at the Indian Agency here, how to address a letter to the Agent at Cheyenne Agency but could get no more than in the papers. I used it—but fear it will not reach the desired Post. I would like to know how and where my Brother

---

[24] Grinnell reported in 1913 that Willie was then living at Pine Ridge Agency in Nebraska. *Beyond the Old Frontier* (New York: Charles Scribner's Sons, 1913), 248–49.

[25] Cheyenne and Arapaho Agency Files, Hoag to Darlington, August 1, 1871.

was buried & the particulars of his sickness & if he left a *will*, all you can learn of him write me.

if C. F. Tracy was Home from Washington he is acquainted with me.

You will please direct to Nancy L. Acks, No. 1222 St., Antony St., St. Louis, Mo.[26]

So the odyssey of John Simpson Smith ended. For those who feel that each man plays a role set for him by fate, it might be said that the time had come for Smith's life to end. The Central Plains, now criss-crossed by wagon roads, railway lines, and telegraph wires, had been conquered by the white man. The buffalo, which was the very heart throb of the old life on the Plains, was in the final stages of being killed off, as was much of the other wild game. Though there would be a few desperate efforts by the Cheyenne to escape their reservation prisons, they were a conquered people.

New settlements were sprouting up daily along the Arkansas, the Platte, the Republican, the Solomon, the Smoky Hill, and all the other rivers where once John Smith and the Cheyenne had hunted in peace and contentment. The giant nation of the white man, its wounds of civil war now healed, grew ever more powerful. The period of the early West was ended.

Like that of the Cheyenne nation, the day of John Simpson Smith had passed.

---

[26] Cheyenne and Arapaho Letter Book, Agents and Agency File.

SMITH WITH INDIAN DELEGATION, 1871

This last known photograph of John Simpson Smith was taken in
New York, 1871, while touring with an Indian delegation. From left,
standing, are Edmund Guerrier, (?), Smith, and Phillip McCusker.
Seated from left, Arapaho chiefs Little Raven and Bird Chief, Cheyenne chief Little Robe, and Wichita chief Buffalo Goad. Smith died
in Indian Territory one month later.

Bibliography

Bibliography

ARCHIVAL PAPERS

Berthrong Collection, Oklahoma University Division of Manuscripts, Norman, Okla.

Campbell, Walter S., Collection. Oklahoma University Division of Manuscripts, Norman, Okla.

Cheyenne and Arapaho Agency Files. Oklahoma State Historical Society, Oklahoma City, Okla.

Cheyenne and Arapaho Letter Book, 1871. Gilcrease Foundation, Tulsa, Okla.

Drips Papers. Missouri Historical Society, St. Louis, Mo.

Fort Supply Letter Book. Oklahoma University Division of Manuscripts, Norman, Okla.

Gerry Account Books. Colorado Historical Society, Denver, Colo.

Sheridan Papers. Oklahoma University Division of Manuscripts.

Wynkoop, Edward W., Unfinished Manuscript. Colorado Historical Society, Denver, Colo.

GOVERNMENT DOCUMENTS: PUBLISHED

Bureau of Ethnology:
Bulletin 152, *Index to Schoolcraft's "Indian Tribes of the United States,"* Compiled by Frances S. Nichols.

House Executive Documents:
No. 41, W. H. Emory, *Notes of a Military Reconnaissance from Fort Leavenworth, in Missouri, to San Diego in California including Part of the Arkansas, Del Norte, and Gila Rivers* (30 Cong., 1st sess.)

Reports of the Commissioner of Indian Affairs, 1824–1872.

Senate Executive Documents:

No. I, "Appendix to the Report of the Commissioner of Indian Affairs" (30 Cong., 1st sess.)

No. 26, "Sand Creek Massacre" (39th Cong., 2nd sess.)

No. 319, *Indian Affairs, Laws and Treaties*, C. J. Kappler, ed. (58 Cong., 2nd sess.), 4 vols.

Senate Reports:

No. 156, *Report of the Joint Special Committee Appointed Under Resolution of March 3, 1865*, "The Chivington Massacre" (39 Cong., 2nd sess.)

War of the Rebellion, Official Records of the Union and Confederate Armies, 128 vols.

GOVERNMENT DOCUMENTS: UNPUBLISHED

Records of the Office of Indian Affairs:
Central Superintendency, Letters Sent.
Central Superintendency, Letters Received.
Cheyenne and Arapaho Agency, Letters Received.
Colorado Superintendency, Letters Received.
Ledgers of Licensed Indian Traders.
Office of the Commissioner of Indian Affairs, Letters Sent.
Office of Indian Affairs, Letters Sent.
St. Louis Superintendency, Letters Received.
Upper Arkansas Agency, Letters Received.
Upper Platte Agency, Letters Received.

Records of the War Department:
Office of the Adjutant General, Letters Received.
Department of the Missouri:
District of Colorado, Letters Sent.
Fort Dodge, Letters Sent.
Fort Laramie, Letters Sent.
Fort Larned, Letters Sent.
Fort Lyon, Letters Sent.
Fort Supply, Letters Sent.

BOOKS AND ARTICLES

Abel, Annie H. *Chardon's Journal at Fort Clark, 1834–39* (Pierre, So. Dak: South Dakota Department of History, 1932).

Annals of Wyoming, (Cheyenne, Wyo: State Department of History, 1929) vol. 6, nos. 1 & 2 (July–Oct 1929).

Barde, Frederick S., compiler. *Life of "Billy" Dixon* (Guthrie, Okla: Co-operative Publishing Co., 1914).

Bartles, W. H. "Massacre of Confederates by Osage Indians in 1863," *Kansas State Historical Collections,* vol. VIII (Topeka: Kansas Historical Society, 1903–04) pp. 62–66.

Berthrong, Donald J. *The Southern Cheyenne* (Norman, Okla: University of Oklahoma Press, 1963).

Chittenden, Hiram. *The American Fur Trade of the Far West* (Stanford: Academic Reprints, 1954).

————, and Alfred Talbot Richardson. *Life, Letters and Travels of Father Pierre-Jean De Smet, S. J., 1801–1873,* 4 vols. (New York: F. P. Harper, 1905).

Christy, Capt. Charles. "The Personal Memoirs of . . .," *The Trail Magazine,* I (June 1908).

Davis, Theodore R. "Henry M. Stanley's Indian Campaign in 1867," *Westerner's Brand Book,* 1945–46 (Chicago).

Ewers, John C. *The Blackfeet, Raiders on the Northwestern Plains* (Norman: University of Oklahoma Press, 1958).

Farnham, Thomas J. *Travels in the Great Western Prairie, the Anahuac and Rocky Mountains, and in Oregon Territory* (New York: Greeley & McElrath, 1843).

Ferris, Warren A. *Life in the Rocky Mountains,* Paul C. Phillips, ed. (Denver: Old West Publishing Co., 1940).

Fossett, Frank. *Colorado: A Historical, Descriptive and Statistical Work on the Rocky Mt. Gold and Silver Mining Region* (Denver: 1876).

Fuller, Harlin M. and LeRoy R. Hafen, eds. *The Journal of Captain John R. Bell, Official Journalist for the Stephen H. Long Expedition to the Rocky Mountains, 1820, The Far West and the Rockies Historical Series, 1820–1875,* vol. VI (Glendale, Calif: The Arthur H. Clark Co., 1957).

Garfield, Marvin H. "The Indian Question in Congress and in Kansas," *Kansas State Historical Quarterly,* II (Feb. 1933).

Garrard, Lewis H. *Wah-to-Yah and the Taos Trail, The Southwest Historical Series,* vol. VI., ed. by Ralph Bieber (Glendale, Calif: The Arthur H. Clark Co., 1938).

Grinnell, George Bird. "Bent's Old Fort and Its Builders," *Kansas State Historical Collections*, XV (1919–22). Reprint brochure.

————. *Beyond the Old Frontier* (New York: Charles Scribner's Sons, 1913).

————. *The Fighting Cheyennes* (Norman, Okla: The University of Oklahoma Press, 1958).

Hafen, LeRoy R., ed. *Colorado Gold Rush, Southwest Historical Series*, vol. X (Glendale, Calif: The Arthur H. Clark Co., 1941).

————, ed. *Mountain Men and the Fur Trade*, 10 vols. (Glendale, Calif: The Arthur H. Clark Co., 1965–72).

————, ed. *Pike's Peak Guidebooks of 1859, Southwest Historical Series*, vol. IX (Glendale, Calif: The Arthur H. Clark Co., 1941).

————. "Thomas Fitzpatrick and the First Indian Agency in Colorado," *Colorado Magazine*, VI (Mar. 1929).

————, and W. J. Ghent. *Broken Hand, The Life Story of Thomas Fitzpatrick, Chief of the Mountain Men* (Denver: The Old West Publishing Co., 1931).

————, and Ann W. *Colorado, A Story of the State and Its People* (Denver: Old West Publishing Co., 1944).

————, eds. *The Utah Expedition, 1857–58, Far West and Rockies Series*, vol. VIII (Glendale, Calif: The Arthur H. Clark Co., 1958).

————, and Francis Marion Young. *Fort Laramie and the Pageant of the West, 1834–1890* (Glendale, Calif: The Arthur H. Clark Co., 1938).

Hazen, W. H. "Some Corrections of 'Life on the Plains,'" *Chronicles of Oklahoma*, III (Dec. 1925).

Hoig, Stan. *The Sand Creek Massacre* (Norman, Okla: University of Oklahoma Press, 1961).

Hoopes, Alban W. "Thomas S. Twiss, Indian Agent on the Upper Platte, 1855–1861," *Mississippi Valley Historical Review*, XX (1933–34).

Hyde, George E. and Savoie Lottinville, ed. *Life of George Bent, Written From His Letters* (Norman, Okla: University of Oklahoma Press, 1967).

Inman, Colonel Henry. *The Old Santa Fe Trail* (New York: The Macmillan Co., 1897).

Irving, Washington. *A Tour of the Prairies* (Oklahoma City: Harlow Publishing Corp., 1955).

Jones, Douglas C. *The Treaty of Medicine Lodge* (Norman, Okla: University of Oklahoma Press, 1966).

"Kansas Before 1854, A Revised Annal," *Kansas State Historical Quarterly* (Winter 1964).

Kelsey, Harry. "Background to Sand Creek," *Colorado Magazine*, XXXIV (Fall 1968).

"Kiowa-Comanche Campaign of 1860," *Kansas State Historical Quarterly*, XXIII (1957).

Larpenteur, Charles. *Forty Years a Fur Trader on the Upper Missouri* (Chicago: The Lakeside Press, 1933).

"The Lawrence Party of Pike's Peakers and the Founding of St. Charles," *Colorado Magazine*, X (Sept. 1953).

Leonard, Zenas. *Narrative of the Adventures of . . .* (Ann Arbor, Mich: University Microfilms, Inc., 1966).

Lowe, Percival G. *Five Years a Dragoon, '49 to '54 and Other Adventures on the Great Plains* (Kansas City: Franklin Hudson Printing Co., 1906).

McGaa, William. "A Statement Regarding the Formation of the St. Charles and Denver Companies," *Colorado Magazine*, XXII, No. 3 (May 1945), pp. 125–29.

Moore, Horace L. "The Nineteenth Kansas Cavalry in the Washita Campaign—An Address by Colonel Horace L. Moore," *Chronicles of Oklahoma*, II (Dec. 1924).

Mumey, Nolie. *History of the Early Settlements of Denver* (Glendale, Calif: The Arthur H. Clark Co., 1942).

Nicholson, William. "A Tour of Indian Agencies in Kansas and the Indian Territory in 1870," *Kansas Historical Quarterly*, III (Nov. 1934).

Parker, Rev. Samuel. *Journal of an Exploring Tour Beyond the Rocky Mountains* (Ithaca, NY: Andrees and Woodruff, Printers, 1840).

Ruxton, George Frederick. *Life in the Far West* (Norman, Okla: University of Oklahoma Press, 1951).

————. Collected by Clyde and Mae Reed Porter. Edited by LeRoy R. Hafen. *Ruxton of the Rockies* (Norman, Okla: University of Oklahoma Press, 1950).

Sage, Rufus B. *His Letters and Papers, 1836–1847, with an annotated reprint of his ''Scenes'' in the Rocky Mountains and in*

Oregon, California, New Mexico, Texas, and the Grand Prairies, Far West and Rockies, vol. V. Ed. by LeRoy R. Hafen and Ann W. Hafen (Glendale, Calif: The Arthur H. Clark Co., 1956).

Sanford, Albert S., ed. "Life at Camp Weld and Fort Lyon in 1861–62, An Extract from the Diary of Mrs. Byron N. Sanford," *Colorado Magazine,* VII (1929).

Sayre, Hal. "Early Central City Theatrical and Other Reminiscences," *Colorado Magazine,* VI (1929).

"The Seige of Fort Atkinson," Harper's New Monthly Magazine, 15, (Oct. 1857).

Smiley, Jerome C. *History of Denver* (Denver: The Denver Times, 1901).

Spotts, David L. *Campaigning with Custer and the Nineteenth Kansas Volunteer Cavalry on the Washita Campaign, 1868–69.* Ed. by E. A. Brininstool (Los Angeles: Wetzel Publishing Co., 1928).

Stanley, Henry M. *My Early Travels and Adventures in America and Asia* (New York: Charles Scribner's Sons, 1905).

Talbot, Theodore. *The Journals of Theodore Talbot* (Portland: Metropolian Press, 1931).

Taylor, Alfred A. "The Medicine Lodge Peace Council," *Chronicles of Oklahoma,* II (June 1924).

Vestal, Stanley. *Mountain Men* (Boston: Houghton Mifflin, 1937).

Wislizenus, F. A. *A Journey to the Rocky Mountains in the Year 1839* (St. Louis: Missouri Historical Society, 1912).

NEWSPAPERS

Cincinnati Commercial, 1867.
Cincinnati Gazette, 1867.
Chicago Times, 1867.
Chicago Tribune, 1867, 1871.
Daily National Intelligencer (Washington, D.C.) 1837, 1844, 1851, 1852, 1867.
Kansas Weekly Tribune (Lawrence), 1867.
Leavenworth Conservative, 1867.
Leavenworth Times, 1858, 1863.
Missouri Democrat, 1867.

Missouri Republican, 1847, 1851, 1867.
New York Herald, 1867, 1868.
New York Times, 1863, 1871.
New York Tribune, 1857, 1863, 1867, 1868.
Rocky Mountain News (Denver), 1864.
Washington Evening Star, 1863.
Washington National Republican, 1863.
Western Mountaineer (Golden, Colorado), 1860.

Index

Index